EVERYDAY LEADER

Everyday Leader

Priceless Leadership Principles that Connect to Everyday Life for the Everyday Leader

Frank Boudreau

ELM HILL

A Division of
HarperCollins Christian Publishing

www.elmhillbooks.com

Everyday Leader

Priceless Leadership Principles that Connect to Everyday Life for the Everyday Leader

Published in Nashville, Tennessee, by Elm Hill, an imprint of Thomas Nelson. Elm Hill and Thomas Nelson are registered trademarks of HarperCollins Christian Publishing, Inc.

Elm Hill titles may be purchased in bulk for educational, business, fund-raising, or sales promotional use. For information, please e-mail SpecialMarkets@ ThomasNelson.com.

Library of Congress Cataloging-in-Publication Data

Library of Congress Control Number: 2019942719

ISBN 978-1-400326686 (Paperback)
ISBN 978-1-400326693 (eBook)

Contents

Section 5   Managing Your Time

Section 6   Others Developing You

Introduction

This book is a collection of leadership thoughts and principles that I know you will connect with in some way. But it isn't intended to be read cover to cover in one sitting. I recommend you consider it like a devotional that you pick up and read a couple of times a week. For things like this I generally set a repeating calendar notice to remind me to spend a few minutes getting a bit of a leadership nugget or shot in the arm, so to speak. You could pick it up daily and read the book in a little over three months. Or you could schedule two days a week and spread it out over a year, so that each nugget or morsel has a couple of days to really sink in as you apply the principle within. Whatever your style is, I know you will get some value out of this book and I trust it will have a positive impact on your ability to lead your team.

How did this come about? I have worked in some type of leadership or management role since the mid '90s. In some I was a little more successful than others. Early in this journey my boss at the time recommended that I read a book called *The 21 Irrefutable Laws of Leadership* by John Maxwell. That began the reshaping of my thinking toward leadership. It began to impact my approach to managing the production department that I was responsible for, as well as other areas of my life. My approach to the position I held at our small local church as a board member began to change. Most importantly it began to change the way I approached my role as husband and father. Not long after that I began to pick up other books on leadership and tried to focus on Christian authors. Their influence being scriptural I began to understand how much the Bible talks about and provides instruction on how to lead. Since then I have read many books, by Christian and non-Christian authors, on leadership and I've been to a few seminars on the subject. It became a passion and I have come to realize how taking hold of the realities of true leadership can positively impact every part of your life. My wife and I used to teach Bible studies and Sunday school classes on marriage that we called, "What the Bible has to say about marriage." Much of what I learned about leadership through the years greatly impacted that teaching. I have taken many groups of leaders through leadership studies based on books that I've read. I've also been a confidant to many business and church leaders over the years, filling roles such as sounding board, advisor, coach, and even mentor. I certainly don't claim to know everything on the subject. I believe that I am a work in progress, like most. I try my best to learn from my mistakes and repeat my successes. I guess the best way to describe me as a leader is that I am a student of the subject, and I simply want to share what I've learned. As I go through the day to day I come across the occasional quote or illustration or experience that I find connects to a leadership principle in some way and my mind begins to process it. Several years ago, I began to write some of those thoughts down and to send them out to a group of friends and colleagues I work with on leadership development. I got some good feedback on them, so I continued to send them from time to time. I saved them and kept adding to them, as well as adding to the list of people I sent them to, until one day my brother said, "Hey, why don't you put that stuff on the 'Net in a blog?" I dragged my feet for quite a while but started to see that my list of quotes and thoughts as well as my list of recipients were growing and maybe I ought to go ahead and put it on the Web. Fast forward a few years and social media flew past blog sites, so I began to post them there. Finally, I decided to close the old blog site, but I didn't want to lose the posts so one by one I moved them over to my computer and then removed the site. Then I began to look back at all that I had written, and I was reminded of something the Lord impressed upon me to do recently. Not long ago I felt the Lord urging me to write a book on leadership. For a while I didn't put much thought into it other than "I'll start that someday." What I didn't realize at the time was that I had already been writing a book—I just didn't know it at the time. I continue to write today so after this book there is much more to come. If you happen to be one of the many who read my blogs or social media posts over the years, I want to thank you for listening and I pray that it encouraged you in some way to continue to grow and give your best to those who you were leading. If this is your first time reading my work, I pray that it will impact you in the same way.

Leading Yourself

Pull the String

"Pull the string, and it will follow wherever you wish. Push it, and it will go nowhere at all."

—Dwight D. Eisenhower

Of course I'm not saying that the people we lead are strings, but what a mental picture when it comes to leading effectively. Think about it, the term "leading" itself infers being out in front.

So many leaders, when the pressure is on, try to "push" the team to get more or better results. Now there might be some temporary desired results, but those are rarely sustained at any level. People will only allow themselves to be "pushed" for so long before they start to either push back or walk away. The best employees will tough it out for as long as they can. They will give you the benefit of the doubt, extend grace and understanding, and do their best to be loyal. They will tell themselves, "Once we get past this rough spot it'll be OK." But even the best have a breaking point. And if you don't start picking up on the signs, you lose them, too.

So get out there in front. Be an example, walk the walk, engage with the team, be the change.

Lead to learn, and you will learn to lead. Be blessed.

Take Action

"Success seems to be connected with action. Successful people keep moving.
They make mistakes, but they don't quit."
—Conrad Hilton, executive

Are you an initiator? Are you constantly on the lookout for opportunity, or do you wait for it to come to you? Are you willing to take steps based on your best instincts? Or do you endlessly analyze everything? Former Chrysler chairman Lee Iacocca said, "Even the right decision is the wrong decision if it is made too late."

"If you haven't pushed yourself lately and gotten out of your comfort zone, you may need to jump-start your initiative."
—John C. Maxwell, author

Be aware of your surroundings. Be alert for what needs to be done and be ready to initiate the action needed to make it happen. If you wait for opportunity to knock on your door, it might be a very long wait. If you think your people need more training, be the first to start working with them and teaching them. If you think your area needs to be reorganized, take that first step and start sharing your vision with your people. If you feel morale is a little low, be the first to smile and say hello in the morning. If you wish your folks would be more helpful to each other, be the first to offer a helping hand. If you see a problem, start today taking steps to correct it.

Don't wait for someone else to do it.

Let's work toward being great leaders and start initiating the kind of actions and activities we would like to see in the people we lead.

Be blessed.

Dare to Dream

"I would rather fail at something I love than succeed at something I hate."

—Mark Batterson, author

Why do we continue to do what we hate to do? Is it obligation? Is it duty? Is it, "I got to do what I got to do"? Maybe we just didn't know we wouldn't like it when we started but it's, "Too late to change now." Maybe we can't afford to make the change.

There are countless reasons why we continue down life's highway doing what we don't like or even hate to do. But is it really worth continuing on that way? The fact is that we pay a hefty price for it. Typically the results are frustration, stress, dissatisfaction, less than excellent performance, unhappiness, drained at the end of the day, and the like. At the very least we simply aren't enjoying life like we had hoped.

Can you put a price tag on happiness? Can you imagine a relatively stress-free life? No matter what you do there will always be difficult times regardless of your occupation or income. The difference is your state of mind when those times come your way and whether or not you are still standing when the storm is over. Are you able to withstand the winds of the storms? Or do you sometimes just run out of energy and collapse in despair and just pray for it to end?

We spend more than half of our waking hours doing the "job." Some say we spend more time with coworkers than family. If that is really the case, wouldn't it make sense to pursue a "job" that is personally rewarding and satisfying? Maybe it's at the same company you work at now but just in a different capacity or position. Does it really matter what your "title" is? I mean at the end of the day, isn't it more important that you were productive and actually got some satisfaction out of what you did for the day?

When you are doing a "job" that you really enjoy doing, the picture is much different. Typically the results are satisfaction, productive, enjoyment, positive influence, excellence in performance, good relationships, energy at the end of the day, and so on. The truth is, you would be adding value to your employer, your life, and the lives of those around you all at the same time.

I'm not telling you to quit your job today. It might take a long time to make a change like that. It could take many decisions over months or even years to put yourself in a position to do what you love to do. But hey, why not try? Even if it took years to get there, at least you eventually get there. If you don't start making small changes and decisions, you'll still be in the same position years down the road. But you'll still be doing something you don't like to do.

Perhaps you aren't sure what "it" is that you would like or enjoy doing. Start trying to figure that out.

Dare to dream and dare to pursue that dream.

Be blessed.

You Get What You Pay For

"No one can do the minimum and reach his maximum potential."
—John C. Maxwell

Have you ever heard the saying, "You get what you pay for"? I'm sure we all have. I also imagine you can recall a time when that loudly proved to be true. I remember standing in the middle of Walmart in front of a row of vacuum cleaners, trying to decide which one to get. Trying to keep a budget I didn't want to spend too much but wanted a good one that would last a while. Hmmmm. You've been there, haven't you? So I'm staring back and forth between the $79 one and the $109 one. $109 was a little more than I wanted to spend but was obviously better quality. As you can imagine I bought the $79 vacuum and I've regretted it ever since. One of these days when I feel I've gotten my $79 worth of use out of it I'll definitely go buy the better one. I sure got what I paid for.

Here is one for you gear heads. Years ago I was building a 455 for my

'68 Pontiac and needed to decide on internal parts. I could buy cast pistons for $179 for the set or buy forged pistons for $379 for the set. Once again I opted for the "less expensive" parts. Within three weeks the nearly twelve-to-one compression in that massive engine destroyed two of the pistons. I replaced the two bad pistons and about four weeks later two more were destroyed. They were literally breaking between the compression rings. I sure got what I paid for. Finally I spent the $379 and bought the good pistons. I never had a problem after that.

The muscles in our bodies are designed in such a way that when we push and stretch close to the limit; they resist and get sore. But then something amazing happens—they actually grow and get stronger. A good athlete will work hard, but the great ones will work even harder and push themselves to the limit because they understand to get the maximum results they have to put in the maximum effort. And you get what you pay for. If you pay the maximum price you will get the maximum results.

Those basic principles apply to leadership as well. It takes effort, work, and sacrifice to grow as a leader. If you want maximum results from your leadership, you have to put forth maximum effort as a leader. That doesn't mean you do all of your teams work yourself. But it does mean that you will have to do all the things a great leader has to do. Ultimately you will get what you pay for. You will reap what you sow.

If you want to be your best, you have to give your best.

Be blessed.

Good Ole-Fashioned Hard Work or Pursuit of Happiness

"All growth depends upon activity. There is no development physically or intellectually without effort, and effort means work. Work is not a curse; it is the prerogative of intelligence, the only means to man-hood and the measure of civilization."

—Calvin Coolidge

We all have a desire to increase in some way. Perhaps you desire to increase financially. You might want to increase in rank or position. What about an increase of joy in your marriage? Maybe you would like to increase in physical fitness. If we really think about it, there are likely many more ways we would like to increase. For example, you might want to have more influence in your leadership. Here is a good one: how about increase in wisdom? I know I could sure use that. Giving it more thought, perhaps you desire to increase your ministry. Maybe you want to increase your skill level in your favorite activity, like sports or writing or painting. There are many ways that we desire to increase that are good and healthy and wouldn't be considered greedy at all. Of course that really depends on the true reason for the desire for increase, which is a matter of the heart.

Well, if you really want to see increase in any of these areas, I'm going to have to break the bad news to you. You're going to have to work. Yes, that's right. It takes good ole-fashioned hard work. Sure there are a lucky few who didn't have to work for something to increase, but just how lucky are they really? I believe that if you work hard for something you will appreciate it much more and you will be willing to put in the daily maintenance needed to maintain it.

If you will put in the work, you will experience increase. It's a basic principle. But there is something I must add, and that is "servant leadership." A good leader understands that to see increase in leadership influence or relationships, there has to be a balanced level of servant leadership. You have to be ready to serve and work hard. If you serve those you lead, they will be willing to serve each other under your leadership. If you can lead a group of people to the point where they truly serve each other, you will see increase in your leadership influence. And that's going to make great things possible.

Teaching Is a Gift, Learning Is a Skill

"In the Western tradition, we have focused on teaching as a skill and forgotten what Socrates knew: teaching is a gift, learning is a skill."

—Peter Drucker

There are a few folks in this world for which learning comes naturally and easily. For the rest of us we need to continuously develop and hone this skill. We spend the first eighteen years of our lives practicing this skill, and if we decide to pursue college or trade school we practice it for a few more years. Then we enter the "real" world where we are challenged to put to use all that we have learned. Typically we experience another learning experience with a new job or career and again are challenged to put together all that we "know." Eventually, though, something interesting happens. Maybe it's our first job that we keep for a long time, or perhaps we've tried a few jobs here and there before we finally find ourselves where we are. Either way eventually something interesting happens. We get comfortable or confident in what we know and what we do. Experience has taken over and we can roll with the punches and take care of the daily tasks that come our way almost without thinking about them. It's kind of like we are on autopilot sometimes. From time to time we are caught off guard or surprised, but we manage to get through and then we are back on autopilot and all is well. Sound familiar?

For many of us who find ourselves in leadership positions at work or church or even leading at the home front as parents, we discover that what we know isn't quite enough to be as effective as we want to be. But we're not quite sure where to turn or what we need to learn. That can be discouraging, so I want to throw another quote at you to fuel more thoughts:

"As long as you're green, you're growing. As soon as you're ripe, you start to rot."

—Ray Kroc

Those are strong words, but if you'll give it a little thought you'll probably agree. The world around us is growing and changing faster than ever before. And if we want to continue to be effective as leaders we are going to have to grow and change with it. Otherwise, eventually, we won't be leading them anywhere at all and someone else will have to take the baton and carry on.

Now we don't have to know everything all at once. We simply need to stay ahead of those we lead. Sure we want to know as much as we can so that we can be effective. But with regard to what we are talking about today, just focus on continually learning so that you always have something new to offer your team. And there is no shortage of information or training. We have learning resources all around us. We can learn from books, videos, coaches, teachers, our peers, classrooms, and the like. And now we have twenty-four-hour access to online reading and videos to learn just about anything we need to learn. You might have to get creative to work with your schedule, but I promise it will be worth it. And the folks who follow you will benefit as well. So do it for yourself, and most of all do it for them.

Keep growing. Be blessed.

"Have We Had This Problem Before?"

"The measure of success is not whether you have a tough problem to deal with, but whether it is the same problem you had last year."
—John Foster Dulles, former Secretary of State

Without a doubt problems will come. Some problems are tougher to solve than others. The question is, do we solve them for good or do we come up with temporary solutions? Do we find ourselves dealing with the same problem over and over again?

Oftentimes we approach a problem and are only able to see them from the surface. Trying to solve a problem based only on what we see on the surface can be fatal. Think of the iceberg. What we see on the surface of the water can sometimes be as little as 25 percent of the total size of the iceberg. And the part below the surface can often cause the most damage (the RMS *Titanic*). What we see on the surface can be very deceiving. Think about the doctor visit if you have a possible broken bone. The doctors can't tell how bad it really is or how they are going to correct it until they see the X-ray.

When we are faced with a problem we have to look below the surface and get to the root of the problem before we can know how to really solve it. If we only deal with what is on the surface, we are only dealing with the symptoms and the real illness doesn't go away. Basically we might only be putting a Band-Aid on a broken leg, or we might only be taking an aspirin for a major sinus infection. The immediate pain might be covered up, but the real problem is still there. Let's take time to dig into the real heart of the matter. It takes more time and we might get a little messy, but we will be able to get to the real issue and then be able to find the permanent solution.

Also, be encouraged to do the hard work up front and early on. If we don't deal with the real issue or illness as soon as we are aware of it, a mild problem can turn into a major problem. Things can get to a point where there is permanent damage that can't be fixed. If we choose to ignore a problem, it WON'T go away and it will only get worse. Sooner or later the real problem will have to be dealt with.

Remember we will all have tough problems from time to time. The question is how well and how quickly we will deal with those problems.

Murphy's Law

"Success or failure isn't defined by whether or not you avoid problems.

It is defined by whether or not you overcome them."

—Frank Boudreau

This thought came to me as I was preparing some training material based on a book by Connors, Smith, and Hickman. In the book they talk about Murphy's Law that says, "Anything that can go wrong, will go wrong." They also talk about O'Reilly's Corollary that adds, "...And at the worst possible time." O'Reilly also said, "Murphy was an optimist." Now that's a dim look at life, isn't it? Of course the writers had a positive purpose and outcome in the use of these quotes in their material, but that's for another time.

The truth is that this world isn't perfect as long as we interact with it. And the more we interact with it, the less perfect it becomes. And as much as I hate to admit it we are the imperfect part of the equation. That being said, people will make mistakes. There will be errors, shortcomings, imperfections, and flaws all around us. Some of them our own doing and some the result of someone else. That's life. So what do we do about it?

We can bury our heads in the sand and ignore or tiptoe around, trying to avoid the issue, but that doesn't change the circumstances. The difficulties are still there, and they are still real. But if we address the problems, work with others to solve them, and forge ahead we will enjoy success. The joy of overcoming far outweighs the drain of the problem. It also helps us realize that this life can be a victorious one. Especially if it helps us prevent the reoccurrence of the same mistake by learning to do things differently next time. As I have said before you must get to the root of the problem if you want to solve it for good. So again, how do you do that? Well, we already know that there are far too many possible problems to list and it would certainly take a lot of paper to detail how to solve every one. Additionally, I would never claim to know how to solve them all. But what I can tell you is that they won't solve themselves, so it will take the following:

- Humility. First things first, go to your bathroom sink and look up. Look in the mirror and ask yourself, "What might have I done to contribute to the problem?" One of the very common setbacks to solving problems is assuming it's always someone else's fault. Look, none of us are perfect so don't expect yourself to be.

- Ownership. We have to own two things. One, own our portion of the problem. Two, own the responsibility to do what we can to fix it.
- Intentionality. You will have to be intentional about getting to the root of the matter, and you will have to be intentional about taking the actions needed to solve them.
- Action. Action can't be overstated. You will have to take the steps. You can't wait for someone to rescue you.
- Compassion. To truly care about others consider how the problem impacts them, more importantly than how it impacts you. Problems are a lot easier to solve with help, and people are much less likely to help if they feel you only care about how the problem affects you.

So keep your head up, link arms with the people around you, and be an overcomer. Take challenges head-on with eyes wide open. Make life count by overcoming adversity and difficulty and then encouraging and showing someone else how to do the same. Real joy in life is helping someone else succeed.

Optimism in the Face of What "Looks Like" Defeat

"Optimism is the faith that leads to achievement. Nothing can be done without hope and confidence."

—Helen Keller

Let's take a look at one of my favorite sports to watch, pro football, and one of my favorite players of all time, the Comeback King, Joe Montana. Why did they call him the Comeback King? Well, let's take a snapshot look back in time. (I'm a true Steelers fan but Joe was the man.)

Trailing 27–21 with 4:54 left on the clock, Montana took the 49ers from their own eleven-yard line to the Cowboys' thirteen in ten plays, including six successful passes and four running plays. Facing a third down at the Dallas six-yard line, Montana made an off-balance pass to the back of the end zone and wide receiver Dwight Clarke leaped to catch the ball for the touchdown. With fifty-one seconds left the 49ers kicked the extra point to beat the Dallas Cowboys and went on to Super Bowl XVI.

In 1989, when the 49ers faced off against the Bengals, Montana produced another fourth-quarter comeback. Trailing 16–13, Montana drove eighty-seven yards and threw the match-winning touchdown to John Taylor with only thirty-four seconds left on the clock. This brings us to Super Bowl XXIV, where the 49ers destroyed the Denver Broncos. The 55–10 score was the most lopsided in Super Bowl history.

Noted for his ability to remain calm under pressure, Montana helped his teams to thirty-one fourth-quarter come-from-behind wins.

Keep in mind the fact that a lot of Joe's great comeback wins were in big games with titles and seasons on the line. Have I got your attention?

How was Joe able to stay so calm under pressure? Well, a big part of it was his level of optimism, hope, and confidence. He would never say, inwardly or outwardly, "We're done." He knew what his team was capable of. He knew the skills of his teammates. And most importantly he had faith in those teammates to rise to the challenge. Many QBs of today and yesterday had his level of skill, but Joe possessed something that most only tried to acquire. That is the ability to stay cool and positive under intense pressure. During the final moments of one of his four Super Bowl wins Joe stepped into the huddle, looked up, pointed to the sidelines, and said, "Hey guys, John Candy is right over there." The incredibly tense moment in the game suddenly subsided. For just a moment his teammates let go of the pressure, looked over at the actor, then back at Joe who was just smiling. Just like that they were relaxed and ready to go. That's what I call being "cool under pressure."

Stay cool, be confident, trust your team, and have faith in knowing what "can be done."

Don't Beat Yourself Up Too Badly

"Too many people overvalue what they are not and undervalue what they are."

—Malcolm Forbes

Man, if I could just think quicker on my feet. If I could only be a better speaker. You know, if I could just have that commanding presence, then I might be a better leader.

Does any of that sound like some thoughts you might have had at one time or another?

Humility is a good quality to have as a leader. It helps us understand that we don't "know it all" and that we need the people we lead. However, an unhealthy level of humility can really take away from the effectiveness of a leader. All too often we put too much stock in the attributes that we don't have, and that can rob us of the confidence that we really need to lead people. It is very important to understand our shortcomings and recognize the areas that need work, but it is equally as important to recognize and understand our strengths. We all have strengths and weaknesses no matter where we are in our development as a leader. That's just human nature.

Sure, you have some areas to work on and there are some attributes that you don't have at this time. But there are likely more areas that you are very strong in and some attributes that are very prominent in you. Recognize and appreciate those areas and attributes of strength. It's perfectly OK to accept where you are today while working on tomorrow. If you don't have confidence in your strengths, how can you expect others to have confidence in you? Besides, if you've been giving the right attention to your team, they will forgive an occasional mistake and be there to back you up.

So cheer up, stand tall, and lead with confidence. Your team needs and deserves a confident leader. You can be that leader for them, so go for it.

Happiness, a Right or a Privilege?

"The Constitution only gives people the right to pursue happiness. You have to catch it yourself."

—Benjamin Franklin

Now this is interesting. We often misinterpret this right and say to ourselves, "I have the RIGHT to BE happy." We get this idea that happiness is due us. That someone owes us happiness. Sometimes we mope around and feel sorry for ourselves because someone isn't making us happy.

But that isn't what Franklin said. He said that we have the Right to PURSUE happiness. Hmmmm. OK, well, I guess that means I have to pursue it. That must mean that it is up to me and I have to work for it. Nobody owes it to me. It isn't due me. It's something I have to work for. OK, that's fair enough, but what exactly am I pursuing? What exactly is happiness? Sometimes we acquire some thing or achieve some goal and think to ourselves that it is supposed to make us happy. And when it doesn't we look to a spouse or boss or friend to pat us on the back or tell us something that will make us happy.

Happiness is different for different people, but one thing is for sure: real happiness doesn't come from an object or recognition.

True happiness comes from relationships. It comes from making a difference in someone else's life. The interaction of people's lives in a positive way. It also comes from accomplishing something greater than yourself, from pursuing something that will stretch and challenge you to grow; something that will cause you to reach further than before.

So to restate something that I'm sure you've heard before, to go somewhere you've never gone you'll have to do something you've never done. Change your routine, do some inward searching, discover something about yourself that needs adjustment or growth or stretched. Go catch your happiness.

Pull the String 2.0

"Pull the string, and it will follow wherever you wish. Push it, and it will go nowhere at all."

—Dwight D. Eisenhower

This is such a simple yet profound truth. Have you ever tried laying a piece of string out on a table to test this? Of course with one finger on one end of the string, if you try to push the string it simply starts curling and wadding up in a pile until you get to the other end of the string. But when you pull (lead) the string it naturally stays in line and follows.

Eisenhower didn't say that we need to keep people on a string. That's not it at all. What he said was if we wish to be a leader, we must be willing to take the first step. If we are expecting our people to improve, we must be willing to improve. If we expect excellence from our team, we must demand excellence from ourselves.

Ask yourself these questions:

Have I gone where I'm asking them to go?
Have I done what I'm asking them to do?
Have I sacrificed what I'm asking them to sacrifice?
Do I model the kind of character that I expect to see in them?

Be gut-level honest with yourself when you ask these questions.

None of us are perfect and we all have areas that need work, so let's challenge ourselves to become better leaders. Then we can challenge our teams to become better at what they do.

Sometimes a leader will get frustrated because his team has become stagnant and doesn't improve or move forward. But all too often the reason for the stagnation and lack of movement is that the leader has become stagnant and immobile. The team can only go where the leader challenges himself to go and therefore can take them.

Man-made Talent or God-given Talent, Which to Pursue?

"There are two kinds of talent, man-made talent and God-given talent. With man-made talent, you have to work very hard. With God-given talent, you just touch it up once in a while."

—Pearl Bailey

While reading John Maxwell's book *Put Your Dreams to the Test*, I came across this quote. In the chapter this quote was referenced, John gave a couple of examples. One of them was when Michael Jordan decided to give baseball a try. Now think about this. Jordan was a phenomenal basketball player and an incredible athlete. If memory serves I think he even played a little baseball in school. It seems like a guy who can achieve such great heights in basketball would be able to transition to baseball and have some success as well. Maybe not quite the extreme as his basketball career but surely some real success, nonetheless. However, his attempt at baseball was mediocre at best. You and I both probably knew guys in high school who could have played better. He batted a .202 and had eleven fielding errors and couldn't get beyond AA ball.

Now Jordan's lack of success wasn't due to lack of effort. He was a world-class athlete. He was well-known for his dedication to practice and training. The difference was that he wasn't working in the area of his God-given talent. He was trying to develop a man-made talent. I'm sure if he were to have spent years training and practicing the game of baseball, Jordan would have indeed experienced some success. Chances are he would have eventually made it to AAA ball; he might have even made it to the pros for a period of time. But it is very doubtful that he would have achieved anywhere near the success that he did in basketball. On the flip side of that I doubt Ironman Cal Ripken, Jr. would have done well on the basketball court, either.

Let's bring this home to the land of the not-so-famous. All this makes me really think about my own God-given talents. Jordan, with the help of his parents, realized his God-given talent and focused on it as most dominant athletes have done. He pursued it and excelled. He also really loved what he was doing. He enjoyed life playing basketball long before the fame and success came so strong.

So what am I doing about my God-given talents?

Am I doing anything to pursue them?

Do I even know enough about them to zero in on one single God-given talent?

Do I know what my most dominant God-given talent is?

If I know what it is, what am I doing to pursue it and further develop it?

What am I doing to position myself to be able to make a living at it?

Doesn't it make sense to pursue it if I can be the most effective and have the greatest impact while using my dominant God-given talent?

Spend some time on this. I know I will. Let's have greater impact, be more effective, and enjoy life more while pursuing our greatest God-given talent.

Be blessed.

The Masterpiece, Who Is Really the Artist?

"When love and skill work together, expect a masterpiece."

—John Ruskin

I want to follow up on the man-made versus God-given talent discussion with this quote. It has been my observation that the masterpieces that we create in life come when we are doing something that we love and are passionate about, and that we have some of that God-given talent to do it. To turn that around, isn't it usually the case that when we are doing what we have the God-given talent to do it is usually something that we also love to do?

When you do what God gave you the talent to do, it is almost always something you truly enjoy doing. I would argue that it's something that you always love doing.

So let me get this straight in my mind. God gave me the talent to do it, and He gave me the passion to do it. And I love it every time I do it. And to top it all off that is when my masterpieces are usually made. Doesn't that make Him the artist instead of me?

Be blessed.

Ready, Aim, Aim, Aim…OK, Shoot Already

"Be willing to make decisions. That's the most important quality in a good leader. Don't fall victim to what I call the ready-aim-aim-aim-aim syndrome. You must be willing to fire."

—T. Boone Pickens

It's a good idea to give thought to your decisions. However, many of us spend too much time thinking about our decisions and not near enough time taking action. I find myself in this category more often than I want to admit. It is important to be ready to make decisions. A very good friend of mine often tells me, "Enough aiming, just shoot." Well, he has a great point, so for those of us who are a little overanalytical, let's be diligent in the pursuit of making educated decisions. But for heaven's sake let's make a decision already.

Don't Get Caught Up in It

"You can't let praise or criticism get to you. It's a weakness to get caught up in either one."

—John Wooden, coach, UCLA

Although sometimes difficult, not letting criticism get to me makes sense. Letting that take root can do a lot of damage. Specifically it can rob me of confidence and dignity. But what about praise? Why would that be dangerous? Don't we all like and sometimes seek it? I admit that I do.

Getting praise isn't a bad thing in itself, but getting caught up in praise can affect some important leadership characteristics like humility, focus, teachability, and others. It can also foster distrust amount your team if they believe you are a glory seeker. They will feel you are in it for yourself and then they won't want to follow you at all. You will have a tough time getting good performance from a team that doesn't trust that you are there for them. So be careful. Accept praise with humility and deflect it to your team. After all without them you wouldn't be getting the praise in the first place.

Be blessed.

How Is Your Conscience?

"Reason often makes mistakes, but conscience never does."

—Josh Billings

With the hustle and bustle of our busy lives we are frequently faced with decisions that will have lasting impact. Although emotion plays a part of the decision-making process, reason also plays an important role. Unfortunately both of them have flaws. I don't know about you but if I make a decision based on emotion, it usually turns out a little rough at the least. Somewhere along the way our conscience comes into play. I believe our conscience is a by-product of our belief system, which is the culmination of our reason, emotions, experiences, and influences through the years. All that being said, if we will listen to our reason, pay attention to our emotions, and balance it all against our conscience, we will make better and more effective decisions that we can live with.

Gotta Get Moving

"Even if you are on the right track, you'll get run over if you just sit there."

—Will Rogers

As an analytical person it is possible for me to get analysis paralysis. I know, you are totally surprised by that, aren't you? Well, it's true. My wife will tell you that on some things I can research forever before finally making my decision. Take a TV for example. I researched LCD versus plasma for months before I finally decided on the plasma (just my personal preference).

Anyway a good friend of mine said I have a habit of…ready, aim, aim, aim…aim some more, then fire if all is perfect and clear. He says, "Just pull the trigger already. If it's wrong, we will fix it later."

Although I thought my method was the "correct" method—you know, get that thing perfectly dialed in on the scope, check the wind and distance, calculate the rate of drop, and so on, and so on—I was typically overanalyzing. I had a hard time accepting the fact that he was right. Take the TV, for example. I ended up selecting the one that I originally thought of buying to begin with. I made my family miss out on five extra months of HD TV just because I wanted to make sure I picked the right one. What a knucklehead.

The reality is that if we get too bogged down in the details and don't get things rolling, we can get run over. Or at the very least get left behind, waving good-bye as the train rolls on down the tracks. So what do we do about it? I'm glad you asked.

First, be diligent and do some homework. Then trust both the results of your homework and your instincts. Finally, make the decision. Don't get caught up second-guessing all of that and find yourself going around the mountain over and over again. Doing that will only frustrate you and, more importantly, the people who count on you to make those decisions.

If you have done your homework and checked your instincts and you still aren't sure, get some counsel from someone who has been there, from someone you trust. Then MAKE the decision. STOP second-guessing. Get on the train, get in the driver's seat once in a while, and push the throttle down.

Yes, you will make a mistake every now and then. But you would have made the mistake whether you ran around the mountain or not. Don't worry too much about that. After all part of your homework should be, "Have I been here before and what were the results?" Which means you likely won't make the same mistake again.

So get moving and be blessed.

Do You Believe You Can Do It?

"The human animal is only driven to the level that their belief system will allow."

—Steve Siebold

Have you ever been discouraged? Or saw someone achieve something amazing and think to yourself, "Man, I wish I could do that"? I know I sure have.

I recently watched the movie *Soul Surfer*. It is an amazing true story about a young woman who was a surfer and well on her way to being a pro. That is, until she lost her entire arm to a sudden shark attack. For the average surfer that would be the end of a career. And rightfully so. But not to the one who believed. She truly believed that she could surf again. And just as important, she had family and friends who also believed that she could do it.

We were created to be able to endure and accomplish incredible things. We all were. So the real question is, do we believe we can? I haven't come face-to-face with a shark. But I came close to losing my arm when nearly 1,000 pounds of glass fell on me. My shoulder muscle was cleanly severed in half and my arm was almost ripped from my body. After several hours of surgery and well over 150 stitches I was put back together. But the surgeon proceeded to tell me that I would lose a considerable amount of the use of my arm. I, like the young surfer, was young enough to believe anything is possible and that I would recover 100 percent. The doc said six weeks to heal, six-plus weeks to rehabilitate, and as much as 25 percent use loss. The result was four weeks to heal, two weeks self-rehabilitation, 100 percent recovery. Doc was a bit surprised, to say the least, and said that if I had taken the easy, slow road to recovery his estimation would have been likely the result.

So does that mean I'm special? No, I just simply believed it could be done and was willing to do the work. Do I believe in divine healing? Of course I do. And I also believe that we were designed in an amazing way with real purpose. And was surrounded by people who believed the same.

What am I saying? Our drive to achieve, endure, survive, and overcome is directly linked to what we "truly" believe (Mark 10:27).

Is a Problem Really a Problem?

"No problem is a problem, except having no problem, now that's a problem."

—Frank Boudreau

Last year in the major leagues the overall batting average was .257. That means they collectively had a 75 percent failure rate. Or is that really failure? A good pro ballplayer will study films of his at bats to look for ways to improve. It's part of the growing process. It's part of life.

Life, like baseball, can throw some serious curve balls, sometimes a changeup or a slider. Yes, that's a problem, but only if we don't learn something from it. I once heard, "If you've had an absolutely perfect day, then you didn't get out of bed." How many can say amen to that? Yep, me, too. Anyway if you had no problems at all, that would be a problem because there wouldn't be much to learn from and there would be nothing to drive you toward growth.

Any inspirational movie fan has heard, "It's not how hard you fall, it's how fast you get back up."

In my line of work I often hear it's not a problem, it's an opportunity.

Are You Ready to Just Do It?

"Knowing is not enough; we must apply. Willing is not enough; we must do."

—Johann Wolfgang von Goethe

To think about it is good. To meditate and plan, even better. But if all we do is think about it and talk about it, we and others will never reap the benefits of our gifts. Yes, we all have gifts and they come in all shapes, styles, and sizes. But if we only think about using them, where is the benefit? If we only talk about it, what's the point in having it? We weren't given our gifts to hide them away or put them in a box for only us to know about them. We were given gifts so that we could use them to benefit those around us as well as ourselves. Don't we teach our kids to share the gifts we give them? Let's share our gifts and make a difference in our world.

Be Yourself

"I'd rather fail at being myself than succeed at being someone else."

—Andre Gide

As difficult as it might be to truly feel this way, if you have tried to be someone you're not, you know how empty that is.

The surprising thing is that we try to be someone we aren't a lot more often than we realize. How often do we force a behavior or a response that is completely out of our normal character? A better question is, why? Why do we feel that we need to be someone we aren't? There are many reasons really. Fear, lack of self-confidence, lack of understanding, lack of faith. Whatever the reason, the results are the same. Loss of self.

The truth is that the only way to truly be successful is to do it as yourself. So maybe you are thinking that being yourself isn't enough. Well, think again.

Remember this, God designed only one you, and He doesn't make mistakes.

Be blessed.

Purpose

In today's fast-paced life understanding purpose is becoming more difficult than ever to determine. Especially individual purpose. Do you still find yourself wondering what you want to be when you grow up?

Yeah, I understand. Believe me.

Well, I wouldn't necessarily say that I have grown up, but I am beginning to close in on my purpose. I wish I could tell you that it is simple. Or that there is a three-step process. But quite honestly it isn't. But I can tell you that it is possible. You just have to know where to look.

Who is the best person to talk to if you want to know the specific purpose for any machine or product? The person who designed it, right? So wouldn't it make sense, if you want to know your specific purpose, to ask the one who designed you? Yes, of course. But it's not your parents. Although they might have an idea, only the designer truly knows. The Word says that He has designed us to fulfill His purpose. So we need to understand Him.

So how do you go about asking Him? You have to spend time with Him and His word. Learn more about Him and how He thinks. The more you understand any designer, the more you understand what he designs.

Also spend some time learning more about yourself. The more you understand the product of the designer, the more you can understand its designed purpose. What are you passionate about? What are your real gifts? What do you absolutely, and purely, love to do? If God is perfect and doesn't make mistakes, and He made us, then we were made for a purpose and on purpose. And if we get to know Him, we will know how to channel our passions, gifts, and abilities toward His purpose for us. And that, my friend, is very fulfilling.

Be blessed.

Will You Learn from Your Setbacks?

"By the end of his military service, Abraham Lincoln had found his rightful place, having achieved the rank of private."

—John Maxwell

It's hard to believe that one of our greatest and most influential presidents failed in his first government leadership position. He was inspirational enough to get a group of men to follow him into service. At that time the person who pulled together a group of men to fight would assume the role of leader, and in his case he was made captain. However, due to his lack of military experience, and his very limited leadership abilities, He would eventually be demoted to private.

Fortunately for all of us, he would learn from this and many other life experiences and become the great president we read about and remember. He would eventually lead this country into a new and defining age that would one day inspire leaders like Dr. MLK.

So the question I will ask you today is, will you learn from your mistakes? Will you be defined by your mistakes, or will what you do as a result of them describe who you are?

Don't be afraid of failure. Be concerned about what you will become if you let failure stop you.

Be blessed.

Can You Light a Fire?

"You cannot kindle a fire in any other heart until it is burning within your own."

—Eleanor Doan

A match has to first be lit before it can light a fire. If you are trying to light a fire in your team and get them moving, you first have to have a fire in yourself. A leader has to be self-motivated. You can't sit around and expect others to motivate you and your team. That is your responsibility, nobody else's. You have to be the motivator. You have to bring the flame to the team. That is what they are looking to you for.

So how do you get yourself motivated? What does it take to get your flame burning?

If you are leading a team and need motivation, think about what you are doing. Now think about WHY you are doing it. What is your reason? If you are doing it because you have to, start thinking about the benefits of doing it. Look for the good in the results of doing it. What or who will it benefit? Find something in it you can get behind and start promoting it.

Motivate yourself to get motivated and that will motivate others.

Does Fear Have You Frozen in Your Tracks?

"I dream of men who take the next step instead of worrying about the next thousand steps."

—Teddy Roosevelt

You know, at one point in time or another we all find ourselves feeling like the "deer in the headlights." Maybe we are tackling a large project around the house that we don't have much experience in. Or perhaps our boss just asked us to tackle a new position or role that we aren't confident in. Or maybe we have decided that we need to get an education to be competitive in the marketplace. Any of these or other scenarios can find us frozen, thinking about all of the unknown things that we are going to be facing. Before you know it "deer in the headlights" and not going anywhere.

Listen, don't let the enormity of your challenge stop you in your tracks. Of course you need at least some idea of the goal (a well-defined goal definitely helps) to keep you pointed in the right direction, but you don't necessarily have to know exactly what you are going to do or face every step of the way. At some point you have to have faith, see the next step, and take it boldly.

Get out there and git'r dun.

Decisions

"When a man has put a limit on what he will do, he has put a limit on what he can do."

—Charles Schwab

We all have God-given talents and gifts. Natural abilities that, when embraced and developed, can have a tremendous impact on our lives and the lives of people around us.

However, the level of impact is completely up to you and me. The only way my gifts and talents are going to benefit anyone, including me and my family, is if I decide to do something with it. It's a decision we have to make. Take a top fuel dragster, for example. If you don't decide to turn the key, you'll never experience the nearly two thousand horse power. All that power is not beneficial if you don't turn the key.

The trouble is that oftentimes we think our gifts have no value. Maybe someone said you're not good enough. Or that you don't have any gifted-ness at all. Perhaps you tried using your gifts and it just didn't work out, so you let it go. Maybe you "don't have time" or the timing isn't right. Whatever the case it isn't meant to be that way.

You have gifts and talents for a reason. And if you want to find out why you have them and how they can impact your world, you have to decide to do something about it. All gifts have to be developed regardless of the gift. It's going to take work, commitment, time, and energy. Most importantly it will take courage.

So be courageous and make the decision to do something different and start the journey today. It doesn't matter how young or old you are. Now is the time. So get started.

Be blessed.

Be a Majority

> "One person with courage can be a majority."
> —John Maxwell

It is interesting how often people will wait for the first person to "step in" or "step up" or "step out." Anxious, excited, or perhaps even nervous, just wishing someone would take that first step. Then they would feel that it is OK to do the same.

Well, leaders "step in" or "step up" or "step out." A good leader will assess the situation, listen to good counsel, and take action. But it takes courage to do so. Remember that courage isn't the absence of fear; it is stepping in, up, or out while facing the very thing you are afraid of. And if you are waiting for someone else to take that first step, you are apparently waiting for the real leader to show up.

Be a majority.

How Do I Fix This?

I pushed my car into the shop. Whew, what a relief. I really didn't know if I was going to make it. But hey, there it is. Worn out from bumper to bumper. Brakes were shot. It rattled in places I couldn't even find. The steering wheel vibrated above fifty mph. And now, after some crazy noises from under the hood, it won't even run.

But no worries now; it's in my shop. And I have an awesome set of tools. You should see 'em. Spared no expense. I even have a bunch of special tools that I barely even remember what they are called. But I got 'em. So by morning the old wagon should be as good as new.

With that I shut the door and headed into the house and turned on the TV.

The next morning I headed out to the shop all excited to see how things turned out. But to my surprise it looked just like it did yesterday. Nothing was fixed. It's like I never even put it in the shop. I don't understand!

Listen, you can have tremendous knowledge, know all the tricks, been to every seminar, and have all the buzz words memorized. But if you can't apply it, or simply don't apply it, nothing will change. In fact knowing just a little bit and applying it is tenfold more productive than knowing it all and applying nothing.

Want things to change? Take what you know and apply it. Then go learn some more and apply that. Make it a journey and make a difference. Be blessed.

Let It Happen or Make It Happen!

"Things can happen to you, or things can happen because of you."

—FB

Let's face it. Things are constantly in motion. That's a lot of moving parts and sometimes (maybe often) it feels like we are getting hit from every angle. That's when things are happening "to" us. We feel we are constantly on the defensive. Not a fun place to be, right?

So how do we get to the place where things are happening "because" of us? That place where we stop for a moment and look around to see the many things that are going on as a result of what we have set in motion. You know, when things are just clicking.

Although it takes some work to get from point A to point B, it all has to start somewhere. And believe it or not that starting point is in the mind. We have to win the mental battle first if we are ever going to have a shot at winning the physical challenges in front of us. OK, so how do we win that mental battle?

- o Don't go it alone – strong peer relationships help you see the blind spots. Trust me, if you are blowing it, the people around you know it. And perhaps before you do. So tap into that resource. A little humility and willingness to learn goes a long way.
- o Get real with yourself – know your strengths and weaknesses. Capitalize on your strengths. Get some help or delegate in your areas of weak spots. (Strong peer relationships really help here.)
- o Hear yourself – think about how you are thinking about yourself. Change from "I can't do this" to "I'm going to find the help I need to get this done." Change from "I don't know how" to "I don't know yet, but I'm going to learn."
- o Own it – listen, we all have things going on that are somewhat out of our control. But you can control how you respond to those things. Your success depends on you taking responsibility for your situation. Take ownership of your path. No one will be as passionate about your journey as you can be. If there is something you don't know, take responsibility to learn it. If there is help you need from someone else, be the one to initiate it.

There are lots of great resources out there to help us get motivated to win the mental battle. Make it your mission to tap into some of them.

Have You Heard the Bell Ring?

It's been said that a day of coasting can eliminate three days of hard work.

The Machine Gun Preacher said to stop focusing on what you've done and start focusing on what you haven't done yet.

I've got to tell you, some days I am just done. Do you ever feel like that? Like you just can't take another blow, another setback or emergency or problem. For crying out loud, enough already.

I believe that is when we find out if we will ever be successful or not. It's the crossroads of decision. Am I going to press on and keep on going? Or am I really finished and throwing in the towel? Success comes in all shapes and sizes, but it never comes easy. And it doesn't happen by accident.

If we are going to reach the goal, make a difference, or turn things around, we are going to have to be committed to the everyday grind until we get there and beyond. We have to be ready to go further than the goal, more than the extra mile, take the long road and then some. It's simply not going to be easy.

So let's do this, let's put in the hard work and go the distance. Let's lean in and lean forward, and even lean on each other when we need to. Let's make the decision to keep going forward.

Be blessed.

How Is Your Level of Engagement?

We must be aware of our own level of engagement. It is a lead indicator of what is to come.

Have you ever pulled into the driveway at home or work and just had to sit there for a minute before you got out of the car? Perhaps you knew you had to have a tough conversation with someone, or things just felt like they were falling apart. Maybe the expectations were mounting and the weight of responsibility was just really heavy that day. We thought for a moment, "I just don't know if I have what it takes," or "I don't know if I can make it through this." At that moment we usually talk to ourselves and muster up the courage to press on. Then we get out of the car, take a deep breath, and start walking toward the door.

Every one of us experiences this at one time or another, and likely more than once. It doesn't make us a failure. It makes us human. It simply means we are going through life.

Now it's what we do after we walk through the door that really matters. If we are not careful, that feeling of inadequacy can cause us to disengage. We can lose focus and stop responding with intention. Or we start putting off the "difficult" tasks and conversations, basically just going through the motions. That is when things start to slip. Then we start neglecting even the little things, which always end up being a big problem.

Or we can recognize the state of mind and make a decision to engage even more, to push through. Get some encouragement from a trusted friend or colleague. It's often during these times when, if we can help each other push on and stay engaged, we get a "breakthrough" and good stuff really starts happening.

So if a friend or trusted colleague says something like, "Hey, you haven't been yourself lately," take notice. Ask yourself if you have disengaged. It might be the signal to wake up, reengage, dig in, and push forward.

Be blessed.

Personal Development

"Personal development is the belief that you are worth the effort, time, and energy needed to develop yourself."
—Denis Waitley

Chances are you have either the training, education, talent, or a combination of these to succeed. Denzel Washington asked a graduating class of the University of Pennsylvania, "But do you have the guts to fail?"

First, you have to realize that you are not on this earth by accident. You are here to have an impact on the people around you. Your unique design and experiences have equipped you to be valuable, and the more you invest in your life and growth, the more value you bring to the world around you.

Second, you have to work up the nerve to try. Have the guts to try and miss. Michael Jordan shot roughly 50 percent. Arguably the greatest basketball player ever, and he missed half the time. In fact he missed twice as many three-point shots as he made. A little over 500 three-pointers, which means he missed over 1,000—yes, 1,000 three-point shots. Most have heard that Edison failed about 1,000 times before success with the light bulb.

Failing is part of growing, as long as you keep trying. Rocky said, "It's not how hard you get hit. It's how hard you get hit and keep moving forward... That's how winning is done."

Be blessed.

Why Change?

"Most people are more comfortable with old problems than with new solutions."

—Charles H. Bower

Change is often hard to accept. Let's face it. Sometimes it's downright spooky. The uncertainty of how things will turn out can leave us paralyzed. One of the big questions is, "How will it affect me"?

But sometimes it isn't the uncertainty of the new solution that holds people back. Sometimes it's the comfort of the old that we just can't part with. Regardless of whether we like the results of the old way or not, we "know" the old way. We know what to expect. We know what to do and how to do it. We know what's expected of us in the old way. I like the knowing. I like the "no surprises."

Well, regardless of the reason, as we have all heard many times if you keep doing what you're doing, you'll keep getting what you're getting. So to answer the initial question—why change?—because it's the only way you are going to get different results. If the results you are getting aren't what you want, you have to make a change. And it might need to be a drastic change that is very uncomfortable.

So get to changin' and be blessed.

How Hungry Are You?

I love to go to gatherings of friends or family. There is always a spread of great food. All kinds of food like chips 'n dip, those cute little triangle-shaped sandwiches, veggie trays, some kind of small bite-size meat with a toothpick sticking out of it, some mouth-watering dessert that we can't pronounce but looks amazing. And it's cool because no matter how hungry we are there is more than enough to eat. I mean if you're not hungry, you don't have to eat anything. Or if you're a little bit hungry, just put a few of your favorites on a plate and nibble for a while. But if you are really hungry, you can pile as much on your plate as it will hold and just sit down and dig in. And if you're still hungry, you can GO back for more. It's awesome!

Now you also hear lots of conversations all around the room of people catching up and telling stories. You hear laughter and chuckling in one corner, a sigh and consoling in another. And depending on the group, you might hear arguing, fussing, and gossiping. And you can engage in as much or as little of any of them as you want to.

Learning and growing are very much the same. There is more information and teaching available to the average person today than there ever has been in history. No matter the subject, if you have any hunger for it at all, it's available to you. If you are only a little hungry, you can "click" here and there for a few of your favorites and just graze throughout the day or week. Or if you are really hungry, you can fill up your plate and start digging in. But if you're not hungry at all, with one push of a button you can just turn it off and walk away. The question is, how hungry are you?

Another question is, what are you hungry for? Just like the food at the gathering there are all kinds of knowledge food to eat:

Filler food. This is the fluffy stuff, the knowledge that kinda just fills you up. It doesn't provide any real value. It just takes up space in your mind.

Appetizers. It's fairly good food that's really a filler to hold you off until the main course gets there.

Main course. The meat and potatoes. The real substance that provides what your mind really needs to grow up good and strong. Lots of value in this.

Dessert. The sweet stuff. No real value. It just tickles your ear and makes you "feel" good about yourself or others.

So what are you hungry for in your walk?

Don't Loan It, OWN IT!

You know we've all heard the saying admit your mistakes. What does that really mean, to admit your mistakes? Does it just mean to say, yeah I messed up and that's it? I mean is it really just about speaking the fact that I made a mistake? While that's important it certainly not going to get you very far with regard to resolution to a problem. And another question is, what are the words that come right after the mistake that you admit? If you're like me, it is, but I'm only human. Or but I was under a lot of pressure. Or but I had to because...

That's not owning it, that's loaning it. That's saying, "Yeah, I did it but it's not my fault, it's someone else's." That's loaning your guilt to someone or something else. There's no freedom in that. There's no weight release when you do that. You're simply loaning the guilt, but you still have the responsibility, you still have to carry the debt.

The Word says we are to confess to one another.

The Word says we are to repent and turn from those ways.

The confession isn't just the act of speaking. It's much more than that. Listen, if you want real freedom from the weight of guilt, you have to accept the fact that you are the responsible party. Truly owning it means understanding and accepting your error. Taking the full responsibility of your actions with no excuses, saying, "It's my fault and no one else's."

Now the repenting part. It's more than just saying, "I'm sorry." No, it's swallowing your pride and finding compassion. Let me explain. Repentance isn't an outward act. It's a heart thing. It's looking at the person you hurt or offended and considering their feelings and how it affected them and owning the fact that you were the cause of that pain. Then finding compassion for that person in their pain. Putting your pride or embarrassment aside. It's deciding to make the healing of their pain more important than our own. But it doesn't even stop there. Now comes the hardest part. Now you have to walk it out in action, speech, behavior, and mind. When your buddy says, "I can't believe they're mad at you about that. It's their fault anyway," how will you respond? Will you still own it then? Will you try to help your friend understand your new perspective and see things differently? That's when the real test comes. That's when you find out if you have truly repented, regardless of your feelings.

So here is the good news. If you will honestly confess your wrong, truly own it, genuinely repent and change your behavior so that you will not commit the same offense again, and walk out that new behavior and mind-set, you will find freedom from the weight of guilt and shame. You will be able to hold your head up and say, "That was then but this is now." And that is freedom.

Be blessed.

Who Made the Decision?

"As the leader, you can and should surround yourself with talented people who have strengths in areas that you don't. But at the end of the day, you still have to lead."

There are a lot of great books out there on leadership. And many of them advise that a good leader knows their strengths and weaknesses and will assemble a team of individuals who each possesses a strength the leader doesn't have. I wholeheartedly agree with that approach as well as the thought process of bringing the team together to discuss options for major decisions. But let me give you a hypothetical scenario.

The leader is uncertain of the direction to take in a decision that will affect the entire group or organization. So he pulls together the trusted leadership team to discuss it and help make the decision. After much discussion they all settle on the direction to go and the decision is made.

As often happens the next day someone approaches the leader and disagrees with the decision and might even have a reasonable argument. What the leader does next is critical and will depend entirely on whether or not he owns the decision that was made. Unfortunately there are some who don't own it. They allow themselves to be swayed from the original decision and suddenly shift directions. Now the team that was originally involved is moving forward with the original decision, only to be blindsided with this new direction. This only breeds distrust, frustration, and uncertainty in the team you put together to help you make the decision in the first place. A good leader will own the decision that was made and hold steady. Now, if the person actually brought new information that the team didn't have when the original decision was made, the leader should reassemble the team. The new information should be brought to the team to then determine if the decision should change.

You Sow It? They Reap It?

The basics of sowing and reaping play out in every aspect of life. If you sow it, you will reap the results. And leadership is no exception. In fact it goes a step further when you are a leader in any capacity.

As a leader it's important to remember that everything you do, everything you say, and every decision you make will have an impact on the people you lead, whether it's good or bad, gentle or violent, fun or boring. Let's think about this in a different light. Imagine you are out on the lake with friends and family in your boat to enjoy some fun, sun, and wakeboarding. Now it's your boat so you are driving and everyone else is along for the ride, including the person at the end of the rope on the wakeboard. As the driver you determine the direction, of course, because you are at the helm. But you determine so much more. You can decide to turn quickly or nice and smoothly. If you turn quickly, everyone better hold on. If you turn too fast and without warning, you're liable to throw someone overboard. You sow, they reap. You can accelerate abruptly or nice and easy. And just like changing direction, if you punch it without warning you'll throw people to the back of the boat and maybe all the way out into the water. Again you sow, they reap. And what about where you go? The farther out to the open waters, the rougher it gets and consequently so does the ride. And if open waters are where you need to go, how you get there matters also. Head directly into the waves steadily or at an angle wide open. One way is a bit of a rough ride, the other might throw people out or even capsize the boat. You sow, they reap. Let's not forget the person on the end of the rope. They are more affected than anyone. The impact is delayed but multiplied. They aren't protected by the bottom and sides of the boat. They are out there alone and hanging on for dear life. You sow, they reap.

The people in the middle of your boat are your leadership team. They are in the seats closest to you. They at least have some knowledge of what your next move is. But if they are surprised, just imagine how caught off guard the people in the front and back of the boat are. They are the frontline folks. They are the ones who make the work and magic happen. And when they are caught by surprise it's a compounded effect and we often lose them. And the one on the wakeboard at the end of the rope, the person who really goes out on a limb for you. The person who trusts you explicitly and unquestionably. Every move you make has a whiplash effect on them. They receive either the greatest joy or the greatest harm.

As a leader it's not JUST about YOU anymore. It's about everyone you lead as well as those who depend on each one of them. And the higher you go in any organization, the greater the impact and the greater the number of the people impacted. Every decision you make, big or small, affects everyone you lead directly or indirectly. You can't only think about how it affects you anymore. You have to consider how it affects everyone on the team and those who depend on each person on the team.

And if you are thinking about the next promotion or level of leadership in your organization, think long and hard, because someone else's life or livelihood depends on it. They will be the ones who will reap what you sow. Sure, so will you. But you have the choice in what you do and how you do it. They don't. All they can do is hang on in hopes they don't get thrown overboard. Their ride will be smooth or rough based on how you lead.

Here is the good news. You can make it awesome, too. You can make it fun and fulfilling. You can make it a learning and growing environment full of opportunity. You can put in the hard work to make it one of the greatest experiences of their lives. You can make all the difference in the world. So don't be afraid; be mindful. They can reap joy, excitement, growth, health, and productivity. Sow it and they will reap it. Sow joy, sow honesty, sow trust, sow life, sow peace, sow commitment, sow communication, sow integrity, sow love. If you will sow these good things, they will reap them.

Sow well. Be blessed.

DEVELOPING YOUR CHARACTER

Ascend by First Descending

"Do you wish to rise? Begin by descending.
You plan a tower that will pierce the clouds? Lay first the foundation of humility."

—St. Augustine

H umility is a highly underestimated quality of a leader. One definition is: a disposition to be humble; a lack of false pride.

Leadership is far more than knowing a skill or understanding a process and cannot be sustained by position alone. In order for us to succeed as leaders we must continue to learn and grow. But growth and learning require a healthy level of humility. Let's look at it in the context of the quote by St. Augustine. When we think of any of the major structures that have been built all over the world we will find that the most important part of the structure is the foundation. No matter how much time or energy we put into what is above the surface for all to see, if the foundation isn't solid the structure won't survive the difficult times. Storms, winds, rains, and earthquakes will bring it crumbling down if the foundation isn't sufficient in size and strength. So, what are the foundational elements to leadership? Many will say it is honesty and integrity. Many will say it is skill and competency. Still others will say drive and determination, or perhaps many other attributes. All of those answers would be in part correct. Let's consider those attributes as the various sizes of rocks and sand that goes into the concrete. I would have to say that honesty and integrity would be the steel reinforcement that the concrete mix envelopes as it is poured into the mold. So where does humility come in? I argue that it is the mortar that keeps it all together and doesn't let go. It permeates throughout the foundation and allows us to continue to learn and grow so that we continue to be effective and relevant.

Humility:

- Allows us to recognize that we are not perfect and have room to learn and grow
- Allows us to see that we can continually improve our skills and abilities
- Helps us acknowledge that drive and determination must come from within but even that requires an outside influence or catalyst
- Requires courage to know that you don't have to be always be right and confidence to embrace who is

Courage, a Fight against Fear

"Far better is it to dare mighty things, to win glorious triumphs, even though checkered by failure…than to rank with those poor spirits who neither enjoy nor suffer much, because they live in a gray twilight that knows not victory nor defeat."

—Theodore Roosevelt

Courage is something that begins inside each of us. It is a battle against fear and failure. Courage isn't the absence of fear; it is pressing forward through the fear especially when failure is a possibility.

Martin Luther King Jr. said, "The ultimate measure of a man is not where he stands in moments of comfort and convenience, but where he stands at times of challenge and controversy."

To some extent we all like our comfort zones. We settle into some kind of routine or familiarity and step out from time to time and consider something new but rarely act on it.

Now let's consider the fact that we are not only responsible for ourselves but also those who we lead. That adds more reason to be extra careful when considering what we might attempt to achieve. That being said, if we are too cautious, we could be keeping our team from achieving the inspiring things that will make our organization reach its full potential. Every great achievement has suffered it's setbacks along the way.

Be encouraged and have courage. Be ready to step out when the time comes for you to do so.

Be blessed.

Bravery

"Bravery is the capacity to perform properly even when scared half to death."

—General Omar Bradley

True bravery is not the absence of fear; it is looking straight ahead and moving forward toward the very thing that you are afraid of. Look we all have to face things that sometimes seem insurmountable. They are the battles that we face. When we find ourselves confronted with something that scares us we have a choice to make. And, yes, it is a CHOICE. We can either choose to face them and move forward or we can choose to turn and run. Two things come to mind when I think of this.

First, have you ever tried to fight with your back toward your opposition? Think about it. It is impossible. You can't see their next move. Even if you could, how would you defend yourself? How about trying to play football with your back toward the other team? Have you ever tried to tackle a guy by running into him with your back? It just doesn't work. If you are going to have any chance at all, you have to face what is opposing you.

Second, if you do run the other way, you are only going to get farther away from your goal. You might try to run around it, but eventually you will be confronted with it again.

We were designed to learn and grow—physically, mentally, spiritually, and intellectually. Those obstacles that we are sometimes so afraid of are the resistance we need to grow in mind and spirit. Our physical bodies need physical resistance in order to develop and grow. The inward man needs mental, emotional, and intellectual resistance to develop and grow mentally, intellectually, and spiritually.

It is often said that there is nothing new under the sun. I tend to agree with that except that the Word says that His mercies are new every day.

With regard to bravery, know this: whatever obstacle you face you are not the first to face it. Many have gone before you and made it through. Even if you need a little help, look straight ahead and press through. Yes, there are things at work that are out of your control. Trust that He will take care of those things as His Word says He will. That is called faith. But with the things that you CAN control, like your responses and your reactions and your actions, stay focused and move forward even if you are afraid. As you continue to do that through life you will develop the ability to perform very well in spite of fear. And that is called bravery.

Be blessed.

Learn to Stop Falling

"A child doesn't learn how to walk; he just learns how to stop falling down."

—Unknown

I realize this doesn't sound much like a leadership quote, but what a simple statement that can be applied to our lives in leadership.

Have you ever watched a child take his first steps? It's really an amazing thing and we'll get to that in a minute, but first let's talk about the weeks leading up to those first steps. Picture it with me. He crawls up to the coffee table and pulls himself up to his feet. He turns to see you grinning from ear to ear with a toy or snack in your hand. He lets go to reach out to you and "plop," he drops to the floor. Hopefully the diaper cushions the fall, but often it doesn't, and it hurts a little bit. After a few attempts he moves his foot sideways a little to stop himself from falling, then plop. Frustrated he then steps back a little to stop from falling, and plop. He even steps forward and manages to stop himself for just a second as he balances, then plop, sometimes mad and crying. Eventually he learns to balance and then step with balance to keep himself from falling again. There he is, laughing and smiling 'cause he finally did it. Awesome, isn't it? The same can be said for riding a bike. But he's a little older and more coordinated, but when he falls it hurts more, so the effort to prevent the fall is more concentrated.

None of us enjoy pain. In fact we sometimes go way out of our way to avoid it. We will often go to extremes to avoid doing something that we think has a remote chance of causing us pain. Well, that's simply a reaction to fear. Something I'd like to cover at a later time. But about that pain that we suffer from time to time for various reasons, isn't it frustrating when it happens? I mean sometimes we get angry because something didn't work, and it caused us some pain. That often leads to the blame game, which is yet another subject. The fact is we don't like it and we certainly don't want to think that we were the cause of it. I know I'm not the only one who feels this way sometimes.

However, some pain can be a very healthy thing. It can drive us, if we'll allow it, to achieve much more—to reach greater heights, to right more wrongs, to grow mentally and spiritually as well as physically. Refocus your thinking to accept pain and discomfort as part of the growing and development process. We need to accept our responsibility in the cause of the pain and work toward getting better so that we don't cause that pain again.

Be blessed.

A Good Leader's Character Is...

"Effective leadership is the only competitive advantage that will endure. That's because leadership has two sides—what a person is (character) and what a person does (competence)."

—Stephen Covey

A good leader's character is many things:

It is a compass by which they navigate.
It is the litmus test for actions that might be taken.
It is the check and balance of actions that have been taken.
It is the thermostat that sets the temperature during conflict.
It is the flag that is raised after the dust settles from conflict (should be a flag of honor raised by those who followed).
It is the beacon of light from the lighthouse.
It is the internal governor in the decision-making process.
It is the driving force behind sacrifices that are made for others.
It is a foundational cornerstone of what a leader is made of.
And it is so much more.

Many have heard me say that good character is doing the right thing even if it costs you personally. If you look at the list above and give it a serious amount of thought, it quickly becomes apparent that it is so much more than that. Good character drives so much of the behavior. As much as I want to write more about this I can't stop looking at this list and thinking that for now that's going to have to be it. In the future, as I learn and grow more, I will break these things down. But for now I will have to let the list speak for itself.

Integrity, Read All about It

"I've always tried to live with the following simple rule:
Don't do what you wouldn't feel comfortable reading about in the newspapers the next day."

—Josh Weston, CEO

Wow, have you ever really thought about this? I mean for the most part I'm sure we can all say we are fairly safe on this, but really? What if anything you say or do could actually be broadcast on the news the next day? What if potentially anyone could hear or read about what you did or said today even in the privacy of your car on the way home, or a text message to your closest friend? Pretty scary thought, isn't it?

I often relate leadership stuff to family situations because I'm a firm believer that the true leader in you is the one who shows up at home after work. You just walked in the door and the dishes weren't done and the dogs weren't fed and you just got off the phone with a friend who was really mad about something someone said, and so on. The real leader, the real character, the real you is who responds to the situation at that exact moment. Oh boy, what if that person was the one who was broadcast on the 6 o'clock news? It makes you think, doesn't it?

Another reason that I often relate leadership stuff to family situations is that I believe the most important leadership position you could possibly have is being a leader in your family, especially as a parent. Your kids that you had, have, or will have are learning from the real you. The one who doesn't get seen at the office or church. That is also where your integrity is really developed.

Integrity is developed on a daily basis by the little things that we think no one is paying attention to. But it is a vital and critical part of a good leader. In fact I believe a leader can be a little short on a lot of different areas but simply can't be short on integrity. If integrity begins to diminish the leader will surely fail.

OK, we are all human, so don't beat yourself up if you have slipped on this one a time or two. But know for sure if not attended to it will severely hinder your ability to lead at the very least and quite possibly destroy your ability to lead altogether. That being said, keep Mr. Weston's simple rule in mind at all times. It may sound a little silly, but it sure makes a lot of sense. And it just might help you keep your integrity solid and intact.

Let the Rubber Meet the Road with Integrity

"Wisdom is knowing the right path to take…INTEGRITY is taking it."

—Unknown

The dictionary says that **integrity** is "adherence to moral and ethical principles; soundness of moral character; honesty."

A person with integrity will actually do the right thing even when it costs them personally. To truly walk with integrity is no easy task. In fact human nature fights against it. Walking with integrity requires many other attributes to come into play as well.

Let's think about a circumstance. Let's say you were working on a project and found yourself stumped on part of it. You are very concerned because you believe that you will be judged by your performance on this project. If you don't come up with a solution, you won't get that promotion or bonus. You happen to talk about it with a coworker and that person helps you with the problem. In fact that person actually unlocked a key component and the project wouldn't be successful without it. "Man, do I tell my boss that I really didn't do this by myself? Will my boss feel that I don't have what it takes to solve tough problems? What if my coworker gets the promotion instead?"

Of course the person with integrity explains to the boss how the coworker solved a key component to the project and should be credited for the effort and input. Now what are the other attributes that come into play?

Humble spirit – the proud would have struggled with giving others credit.

Courage – the fearful would have been too worried about what the boss will think.

SelfLESSness – a selfish person would want all the credit.

Honesty – a dishonest person would have lied about it.

Character – a person without character would have had an "I'm gonna get mine" attitude.

We could go on but we'll stop there.

The Bible also has a lot to say about integrity. Several of the verses associate integrity with a characteristic of the heart. It also has a lot to say about the person who walks with integrity.

Job 4:6 (ESV): "Is not your fear of God your confidence, and the integrity of your ways your hope?"

Job 31:6 (ESV): "Let me be weighed in a just balance, and let God know my integrity!"

Psalm 7:8 (ESV): "The LORD judges the peoples; judge me, O LORD, according to my righteousness and according to the integrity that is in me."

Proverbs 2:21 (ESV): "For the upright will inhabit the land, and those with integrity will remain in it."

Proverbs 10:9 (ESV): "Whoever walks in integrity walks securely, but he who makes his ways crooked will be found out."

Proverbs 28:6 (ESV): "Better is a poor man who walks in his integrity than a rich man who is crooked in his ways."

Proverbs 28:18 (ESV): "Whoever walks in integrity will be delivered, but he who is crooked in his ways will suddenly fall."

Does What You Say and What You Do Line Up?

"What People say, what people do, and what they say they do are entirely different things."

—Margaret Mead

I'm fairly confident that we've all met, or know, someone who falls into this category. Basically someone whose actions don't line up with their words. And when you hear them talk about their actions even that doesn't line up. To hear them explain themselves you're thinking, "OK, that's not what I saw or heard you say at all." It's really hard to trust someone like that, isn't it? I mean you never know what to expect out of them. Except that you can't expect them to do what they say they are going to do.

Isn't it important that your words and your actions line up? And that when you describe to someone what you have done or will do, it is accurate and true whether good or bad? The fact is it doesn't take long to identify those who struggle in this area.

In leadership your ability to be believed and trusted is invaluable, even if it costs you.

Honesty and integrity are absolutely imperative to your success as a leader. And to have it you have to pay a price. Sooner or later doing the right thing is going to cost you. However, not doing the right thing will bring a much greater cost. It takes a lifetime of commitment to be the kind of person whom people trust and believe in. But it doesn't take much at all to destroy it.

So do a self-check every once in a while. Have you found yourself trying to lessen what you did wrong? Have you suddenly realized that you just embellished the truth a little to make yourself sound better? Do you find yourself avoiding certain subjects because you feel a little guilty about something you did or said?

Hey, we all make mistakes and none of us are perfect. We all have highs and lows, good seasons and bad. So when your self-check uncovers something, find that person you trust the most who will talk straight with you and talk about what you found. Decide what you need to do to fix things or shore them up. Then recommit yourself to staying on track. Sometimes it takes a little while to regain the confidence in yourself and others, but it's well worth it.

Forever Strong

"It's not about rugby, it's about young men. It's not about building championship teams, it's about building championship boys, boys who will be 'forever strong.'"

—Larry Gelwix

OK, first off, a movie was made based on Coach Gelwix and his rugby team. *Forever Strong* is a very good movie and I recommend it.

Coach Gelwix knew that inner strength is forever strong. Focus on the inner man (the spirit man), develop his character, his discipline, his moral compass, his values, and his ability to listen. Do these things and the outer man (the physical man) will be able to contribute far more to the family, the team, and himself.

Now don't get me wrong. The coach worked the physical man with tough conditioning and focused physical discipline. But he understood that one has to take dominion over the other, and to be a true champion the inner man has to take dominion over the outer man. If it is the reverse, the true champion is suppressed.

Coach said he had only one rule for his players: don't do anything that will embarrass yourself, your team, or your family.

OK, what does all that mean to you? Inside each one of you is a true champion. You see, God doesn't make mistakes, and he made you. You were designed in such a way that if your inner man is developed and disciplined and takes dominion over your outer man, the true champion comes to the surface. A true champion is others focused and has a lasting positive impact on his surroundings. A true champion disciplines himself and puts his energy, efforts, and resources into seeing to it that those around him succeed.

Invest your energy, efforts, and resources into the lives of those around you. Make a difference in their lives and they will make a difference in yours.

Now I'm not talking about being a doormat or a pushover. I am talking about being a strong person on the inside so that you can feel confident about investing in others. When you are strong on the inside you won't worry about being less than, or that investing in others will take away from who you are. Remember no candle loses anything by lighting another candle.

Besides, the coach's philosophies led his Highland Rugby Team to a record of 361 wins and only nine losses. With a record like that, Coach Gelwix's methods must have some validity.

You Get Paid What You Work For

"If a man performs no more service than that for which he is being paid, then obviously he is receiving all the pay to which he is entitled."

—Hill

Hmmm. OK, first of all, if you are in leadership for the money, my best advice for you is to get out as quickly as you can.

Let me clarify that. Of course we all work to earn a living and provide for our families, as we should. However, if you are in "leadership" for personal gain only, it will be an uphill climb all the way and reaching your full potential will be extremely difficult.

Success in leadership takes much more than the list of things that your boss tells you to do. Doing just enough to get by will never be enough to be an effective leader. Over the last couple of years we have talked about many of the things that it takes to be a good leader, and I hope to talk about more of those things. There are characteristics and qualities; there are skills and practices that are required to be a good leader.

Well, if it takes so many qualities and so much work, what motivates us to do all that? That brings me back to my first statement. Money just isn't the right kind of motivation for true leadership because true leadership requires strength in matters of the heart. You have to care about more than yourself. You have to want to make a difference in the lives of others and in your organization, and doing just enough to get by won't make much difference, will it?

Here is another thought: if you are only doing "just enough to get by," you will only ever make "just enough to get by." It doesn't matter who's fault it is or isn't. That is simply a basic truth, that 99 percent of the population can't get around.

Why Do We Stand By?

"All that is necessary for the triumph of evil is that good men do nothing."

—Edmond Burke

What a simple but profound statement. Most people refer to this timeless quote when addressing freedom and liberty, and for good reason. Today I would like to refer to it in regard to leadership.

Why do we so often stand by and do nothing about a wrong act or situation? Is it that we feel that it is none of our business? Do we think that we are powerless to do anything about it? Do we feel that it would be hypocritical to correct someone on something that we do ourselves (ouch)?

Have you ever found yourself thinking, "Man, if Fred (fellow manager or supervisor) saw what his people were doing, he would flip"? Or have you happened along a conversation between people who were trash talking one of the other leaders in the organization and you just kept on going by without saying anything to stop that behavior?

Doing nothing about a wrong act or situation is just about as bad as engaging in it. Let's put it into perspective. I'm certain that if you were to encounter a stranger abusing a child and no other adults around to stop it, you would do "something," right? Of course you would. Although that is an extreme example the principle applies to just about any situation. If you were the one being treated badly, or being talked about, you would want someone to step up and be your advocate, wouldn't you? If it were your employees engaging in wrong behavior while you weren't around, you would want another leader to step up and step in, wouldn't you?

Ignoring wrong acts or behavior won't improve the environment that you work in. In fact it will only enable the environment to continue to spiral downhill and encourage the same behavior in others. However, doing the right thing will invoke improved environment. As a matter of fact, if done consistently, it will encourage the same behavior in others.

I know that taking action can often be very uncomfortable or even a little scary, but it eventually gets easier.

As you know, you reap what you sow. But you can also reap what you "allow to be sown."

Self-Discipline—a Critical Piece of the Leadership Puzzle

"Hold yourself responsible for a higher standard than anybody else expects of you. Never excuse yourself. Never pity yourself. Be a hard master to yourself—and be lenient to everybody else."

—Henry Ward Beecher

Of course there is a level of this that can be too much. That is the point you become self-critical. An extreme in this area can be destructive and send you into a downward spiral. But that is usually the result of unrealistic standards. It's when you put demands on yourself that aren't humanly possible.

However, as a general rule self-discipline is very important to leadership. It is important to living a healthy life, for that matter. If you are going to go the distance, self-discipline is a primary tool. We all know that settling down and accepting status quo can sometimes be very tempting to do. Let's be real. Sometimes we just want to coast. Sometimes we just want to kick back and take things as they come. I know I struggle with that from time to time. The problem with that is it can easily leave us with our self-check guard down. We can easily be a target for the complacency arrow, and that is destructive. Getting rest at the right times is very important; we will talk about that later. For now we are talking about guarding ourselves against falling into the rut.

So stay engaged. Be disciplined to doing what needs to be done even when nobody expects you to do it. Hold yourself to an achievable but high standard that stretches you. Know that you will make mistakes but don't excuse them. Own them and work hard at correcting them. Don't sit back and just say, "Oh well, I tried. That's all anyone else would have done." Dig deep, fix it, and move on.

The latter part of the quote talks about being lenient to everyone else. Another subject for later but it doesn't mean you let your team get away with everything. Accountability is still necessary, just don't beat them up over every little thing.

Be blessed.

Are You Tough?

"Tough times don't last, tough people do."

—Gregory Peck

When times get tough you find out what you are made of. That is when your true character is revealed. It is also a time to find out what areas you need to work on, but we'll cover that another time.

For now I want to talk about what it means to be tough. Many will say that being tough is being stern, direct, aggressive, and being able to take tough news. I'll have to say that those are good qualities to have and have their place at the right time. But I would submit that there is a seldom recognized trait that requires real toughness. "Consistency."

Consistency in a crisis is critical. It is easy to waiver or shift when the pressure is on. But staying consistent and steady under pressure takes real mental toughness. To keep your emotions under control so that you don't create more problems in the wake of the disaster takes a stable and tough approach.

So are you tough? Do you stand firm and unwavering when you are accused? Do you keep your cool when things go wrong? Are you steady when someone lets you down? Or does a different you come to the surface when these things happen?

Be tough, and be blessed.

Discipline Pushes Champions Past Pain and Punishment

"It's easier to activate yourself into good thinking than it is to think yourself into good action."

—Bill Gove

In some areas of my life discipline comes easy. For example, brushing my teeth every morning after the bowl of reasonably healthy cereal and 2 percent milk. Daily talks with the Lord throughout the day. Daily reading the Word. Telling my wife every day that I love her. Well, you get the picture. We all have things that we do every day that we believe are good for us. And we probably have things that we are sure not to do each day that we feel would not be good for us. Anyway those things we do each day, do they really represent discipline? Or have we been doing them long enough that they are now habits?

Let's be real. These things that we do easily because we've been doing them a while, they are habits. They are good things but they are habits. So let's be careful that we don't throw out a shoulder, patting ourselves on the back for doing them.

Shifting gears, quite often I determine in my thinking that I am going to get back to a regular exercise. Then when I do finally get on the elliptical or treadmill I am quickly reminded why I hadn't started doing that yet. The truth is I am having a hard time converting desire into action. I know I need to. I know it's good for me. And I really want to do it. The simple reality is that I have not been "disciplined" enough to push through the pain and suffering to the point that it becomes a habit again. They say that if you do something for twenty-one days it becomes a habit. Well, even if it took a little longer, it's worth it.

Let's face it. If it's easy, it doesn't take discipline. But if it's tough and it does take discipline, it's bound to be worth the effort.

Now the same thoughts can be applied to anything in life that should be done but is tough to do. It will take discipline to start and keep it going long enough to become a habit. But that's what it takes to keep moving forward, to keep learning and growing, to become a champion. If all you do are the things that are already habits, you are just maintaining at best. Be blessed.

Do You Have Self-Control?

"One can have no smaller or greater mastery than mastery of oneself."

—Leonardo da Vinci

Titus 1:8 (NIV): "Rather, he must be hospitable, one who loves what is good, who is self-controlled, upright, holy and disciplined."

2 Peter 1:5–6 (NIV): "For this very reason, make every effort to add to your faith goodness; and to goodness, knowledge; and to knowledge, self-control; and to self-control, perseverance; and to perseverance, godliness…"

Galatians 5:22–23 (NIV): "But the fruit of the Spirit is love, joy, peace, forbearance, kindness, goodness, faithfulness, gentleness and self-control. Against such things there is no law."

Proverbs 16:32 (NIV): "Better a patient person than a warrior, one with self-control than one who takes a city."

Proverbs 25:28 (NIV): "Like a city whose walls are broken through is a person who lacks self-control."

1 Timothy 3:2 (NIV): "Now the overseer is to be above reproach, faithful to his wife, temperate, self-controlled, respectable, hospitable, able to teach…"

I really don't see the need to add anything to these quotes. Be blessed.

What's Waiting to Boil Out?

"Circumstances do not make the man, they reveal him."

—James Allen

Take a gallon jug of milk and paint it in any color. Paint it to look like a gallon of pickles. Dress it up with different labels. Change the appearance any way you want. But when you squeeze it under pressure and the top pops off, milk is what is coming out.

Circumstances create pressure. Sometimes positive pressure, sometimes negative pressure, but pressure just the same. Regardless, when the pressure increases, and it will, whatever is inside you will definitely come out. It doesn't matter what you try to make yourself look like or how you act.

So let's focus more on what is on the inside and don't worry about what's on the outside so much. Let's develop the inner man and do some cleanup work there.

Be blessed.

With Power Comes Responsibility

"Nearly all men can stand adversity, but if you want to test a man's character, give him power."

—Abraham Lincoln

Being placed in a position of leadership can sometimes feel powerful. Let's face it. It can feel good being able to call the shots. Once you have the title, calling the shots is easy. The hard part is calling the right ones. The real test of character is whether or not you choose to do the right thing even if it costs you something.

The power of position should bring a sense of heaviness, responsibility, humility. A weightiness, not of overburden but of care and concern for the well-being of those in your charge. Your decisions will without a doubt impact them. Either positively or negatively. You will either build up or tear down. The choice is yours.

So with power, how will you decide? Will you place their needs above your pride? Will you place their cares above your own?

You have the power in your decisions. What will you do with that power?

Be blessed.

Trust—You Can't Lead Without It

"Leadership is a potent combination of strategy and character.
But if you must be without one, be without strategy."
—General H. Norman Schwarzkopf

Leaders build trust by consistently demonstrating competence, connection, and trust. People can be patient as you develop competence in areas and develop abilities. They will give you some time to connect with them. But they won't trust someone who has slips in character.

People can overcome errors in strategy. Especially if you have built a relationship with them. But slips in character will negate strengths in any other area. Character makes trust possible and trust makes leadership possible.

Character is consistency. A leader with character can be counted on day in and day out.

Character is potential. No leader can go beyond his character. Simply isn't possible.

Character is respect. Earn their respect and you can earn their trust.

If people can trust you, they will follow you. If they can't, they won't. It's that simple.

Earn their trust and be blessed.

What's Your Motivation?

Are we more concerned about where we are going, or what we are becoming?

This is an interesting contemplation. There needs to be a proper balance, but:

If I am more focused on where I am going, the goal becomes the focus. Whatever the goal is. It could be a promotion, going to the next level, starting my own business, and so on.

If I am more focused on what I am becoming, my image can become the focus. Who I am, how I appear to others, the position or title I have or striving for, and the like.

Hmmmm. So How do I find real balance? And more importantly do any of those things really matter in the grand scheme of things? Well, I suppose in proper perspective all of those things can be important. So what's it really all about? What really is my motivation for any of it?

My answer became "the people." At the end of the day I found that "positively impacting the lives of others" to be my motivation. It's my motivation for striving for higher levels both in where I am going and what I am becoming. I have found myself reaching higher and stretching further so that at each plateau I have more to offer those I am trying to positively impact. I can't give what I don't have.

Consider what your motivation is. Why do you do what you do?

DEVELOPING OTHERS

Money, a Means or an End?

"Organizations are far more interesting when profit is an instrumental value, pursued for the sake of some other values."

—Peter Drucker

Much of our thinking about ethical issues in business is based on our **values**. Values represent our desires and can be either good in themselves (**intrinsic values**) or a means to other ends (**instrumental values**). Values serve as both the reasons for and the causes of many of our actions. It is relatively important to know whether a value is intrinsic and worth pursuing for its own sake or instrumental and likely to lead to or be an indicator of something more important. Some business thinkers (for example, Peter Drucker) have argued that a common mistake that managers make is to assume profit is an intrinsic value to be pursued in its own right (*The Portable MBA*).

Of course business is in business to gain a profit, but why? Why do we really pursue profit anyway? What is it to be used for? Well, let's think long term.

If it is for personal gain and satisfaction, there is nothing specifically wrong with that. However, what will you leave behind and who else can benefit?

If it is for the purpose of providing for the family, an instinctive drive for the average family man/woman, there will be lasting results and some long-term benefits. And the personal gain will occur as a by-product.

If it is for the purpose of providing and supporting of others, well, many will benefit; the family will inherently benefit as well as you.

In conclusion if your intrinsic values are "others" focused, and if you view profit as an instrumental value pursued to be used as an instrument to support the intrinsic values, the benefit will be felt by many and for a very long time. And the journey will be far more interesting, enjoyed by many more people.

Giving Is Part of Good Leadership

"No person was ever honored for what he received.
Honor has been the reward for what he gave."
—Calvin Coolidge, for American president

When faced with an opportunity to give in any way, whether it is time, talent, money, or possessions, something on the inside has to happen. Priorities and perspective come into play.

If the decision to give is easy, it is likely to be one of two reasons. Either what you are giving is a very small portion of what you have or your priorities are such that a sacrifice on your part is well worth the positive impact on others.

Now if the decision to give is difficult, it is likely to be one of these two reasons. Either the cost is so great that the price is too much to bear or your priorities are such that the positive impact on others is not worth a personal sacrifice.

Please understand I'm not talking about giving your house away when you have a family to take care of. I'm not talking about giving all your money away when you have bills to pay and a family to feed.

A good leader needs to understand the value of giving, especially when it costs you something. When there is personal sacrifice with the right attitude it has a lasting impact on your people.

People will follow a leader who is willing to give of himself, someone who genuinely wants to make a positive difference in the lives of others. When the people you lead know your heart as one who gives of self, they will be able to accept the times when you have to have that tough conversation with them for the sake of growth and learning. It's really human nature. If you know that your boss genuinely cares about you and shows that by giving of himself and sacrificing his time and energy, you are far more likely to accept it when you need to be disciplined. Let's face it. We all need a swift kick every once in a while.

If you really struggle with giving, ask yourself this: "Am I satisfied with what I have, or am I constantly in pursuit for more?" If you are constantly in pursuit for more, honestly challenge your perspective of where you are and what you have. Take a good look at your life and you might find you have more to be thankful for than you realize. Our world is a constant bombardment of reminders of what's out there that we don't have. We have to stop for a minute and think about what we do have.

Final thought: to be a true giver you have to find and appreciate the true joy and satisfaction in seeing others grow and prosper. When that is a true desire in your heart, giving becomes easy.

Hard to Say No?

Sometimes we get overwhelmed with tasks and time-consuming discussions simply because we have a hard time saying no. Or is that really it?

Busy life is not hard to accomplish these days. It seems that we all get a little busy, or a lot busy. Either way it seems normal to be busy now. But even among the busy there always seems to be the person who is "super busy." Always running behind. It's that "old reliable" person who so many people lean on to help in a crunch or pick up the slack. I'm not talking about the typical helpful person. I'm talking about the person who "puts on a happy face" to mask the dread and exhaustion of never catching up because of everyone else's stuff they are always helping with.

If that isn't you, you probably know that person. The person who never says no, but never seems to get things finished. Or if they do, it was at the eleventh hour with their hair a mess and jittery from four cups of coffee to try to "keep it going."

So why do they find it so hard to say no? I read that oftentimes it's because they like or need to feel needed. Or they want to feel important. And I suppose that might be the case at times. But I consider that it could be something else. I think that sometimes the person is looking for someone or something that makes them feel appreciated. That there might be someone out there who actually appreciates their hard work and self-sacrifice. If someone would do something that just says thank you as they take, I mean receive.

If that were the case, what can you do about it? What if, rather than asking them for help with something, you were to ask them to let you help them with something, even if they resisted? If you know the person well enough, you might even be able to simply jump right in there and give a helpful hand without being asked. Even more impactful, consider this: rather than thanking them for what they do for you, find a way to express your appreciation for them as a person. A good leader can recognize when a person struggles with saying no. A great leader has the confidence and compassion to take action. After all don't we all want to know that people appreciate us for who we are and not just for what we do?

If you are that person described above, I encourage you to consider your true value. You are unique. You have gifts and talents. You have skills and abilities. You have values and beliefs. You have experiences and you have dreams. Combine all of those things and connect them to what you are passionate about and you just might be able to see your real value. Most people will find it difficult to value you higher than you value yourself.

You have to take the lead. Be confident in who you uniquely are. There is no one exactly like you so don't expect yourself to be like everyone, or anyone else. If you spend time evaluating all of these things and you still struggle with seeing your value, consider how the Creator sees you. If you aren't sure how He sees you, get a copy of His Word and just start reading. Nobody knows the creation better than the Creator. The more you get to know Him, the more you will understand what He created, and that's you.

Who's Career Is Important, Yours or Theirs?

"A good manager is a man who isn't worried about his own career but rather the careers of those who work for him."

—Henry S. Burns

As a manager your greatest resource is the group of people around you. It isn't the building, it isn't the equipment, it isn't the bank account—it is the people. Your people.

They have the greatest impact on success and failure. They have the greatest impact on the P&L statement. They have the greatest impact on you as a manager. And they have the greatest impact on you as a person.

Now here is a side note. If you have been in management or owner- ship for any length of time, you realize that many people will come and go in your organization. It is a fact of life. People move, grow, fall back, loose interest, and many other things that take them from one job to another. The people who work for you are not going to be with you forever.

So with that being said, why should we invest in the careers of our people, especially since they aren't going to be here forever?

Firstly, it will improve them while they are with you and you will reap the benefits.

Secondly, you will improve as it is readily known that the teacher learns as much as the student.

Thirdly, pouring into someone with the right heart fosters contentment, security, enjoyment, and multiplication.

Multiplication brings another reason. As your people become receptive to your pouring into them, encourage them to do the same for their direct reports. When they trust you and what you are doing for them, they will be more likely to pass it on to others and ultimately create an organization of mentorship and development.

On another side note, be ready for some real changes in your organization if you do this. If you are already doing it, you know what I'm talking about.

Besides, I think I read somewhere that we should treat others as we would have them treat us, or something like that. Hmmm... (Luke 6:31). I think there is definitely something there, don't you? I mean don't you hope that someone is willing to invest in you? Or maybe someone already has.

Lead a straight path. Be blessed.

Do Your Actions Inspire?

"If your actions inspire others to dream more, learn more, do more and become more, you are a leader."

—John Quincy Adams

Words can be very inspiring. They can move our emotions and they can muster our courage to take a step. But after that step we are on our own. Well, there is great reward in inspiring others to take a first step by our words. It is good to see that you have moved someone.

However, your actions can move someone far beyond that first step. Your actions can inspire someone to take an entire journey. And it can be done with very few words, if any.

Live a life that inspires. Walk a walk that encourages others to do the right things.

Be blessed.

Get Them Involved

"Show me and I'll see, tell me and I'll hear, involve me and I'll understand."

—Chinese proverb

A leader will tell his people his vision and what he expects. A good leader will tell them and then show them so they can see what his vision is and what he expects. A great leader will not only tell and show but actually involve and empower his people so that they will hear it and see it and fully understand it and how do it. So why is that so important? And why is it so difficult for many of us to do?

As you develop as a leader you will go through many stages of growth. I like to sum up these stages into three statements:

"Look at me."
"Look at us."
"Look at them."

Think about these three statements. Consider what they really mean to you. Then be completely honest with yourself and decide which stage you are in. If you are in the "Look at them" stage, consider how you might be able to continue to improve in that area. If you are not, consider how you might be able to get to that stage.

Be blessed.

First Know, Then Do, So You'll Understand, Then You Can Teach

"Those who know, do. Those that understand, teach."

—Aristotle

The best path to being able to teach someone something is by learning then doing, then doing it some more, so that you actually understand it, then you might be ready to actually teach it.

Way too often we learn about something by reading about it or hearing about it and assume we are the person to teach on the subject. But the reality is, without experiencing it, we really shouldn't try to teach it. Whatever the subject is. So before we try teaching, let's do. And let's do often enough that we really understand first. Then we might be ready.

CPI Requires CPD

"Continuous Process Improvement Requires Continuous People Development."

—Frank Boudreau

You just won't get the one without the other.

After spending years in organizations in either or both people development and process improvement I have come to the above-mentioned conclusion. For several decades or more organizations have been striving to improve their processes in order to stay competitive in the marketplace. But the fact is **people** improve processes. Simply put, the best way to invest in improving your processes is to invest in developing your people. Of course you'll need to invest in process improvement, but with highly developed people you'll have a whole team working on your processes.

An added benefit is that you will have an environment where good people will thrive and be energized by problem solving and accomplishments. Also investing in the development of your people adds stability and improves retention, because people will far more likely stay at a company they feel values them by investing in them. In today's workplace people want to know that they are valued and appreciated. And let's face it: at home we all invest in what we value—our families, the house, the vehicles, hobbies, and so on. We invest in what we value. Well, if we invest in what we value, isn't it reasonable to think that our teams would feel valued if we invest in them?

Be blessed.

Don't Go It Alone

"It's lonely at the top, so you'd better take someone with you."

—Maxwell

So let's explore this for just a minute. We have all heard the saying, "It's lonely at the top." And if you have had any position at or near the top of any organization, group, or business, you have likely felt that very lonely feeling. Especial during difficult times. But does it really have to be that way?

Although there are certain decisions and tasks the leader has to decide or perform on his own, it definitely doesn't have to be lonely. It is important to develop an inner circle of individuals you trust and respect. Not for the purpose of being secretive or exclusive, but to both develop those individuals and to provide the support you need in difficult times. And there will be difficult times; it is inherent in the role.

The support is critical to your ability to be effective in leading and problem solving.

Developing your inner circle is critical to your ability to expand your influence and grow as a leader.

Some might say, "I don't have time to coach and develop the leaders on my team. I shouldn't have to develop them and I simply have too many irons in the fire."

Well, here is what I know: if all YOU do is fight fires, all you will EVER do is fight fires. At some point you have to do some fire prevention. And one of the best ways to prevent future fires is to develop your team.

Be blessed.

What's Really More Important to You?

"…I was not interested in flattery or fluff. Rigidity gets in the way of creativity.
Instead of salutes, I wanted results…"
—Captain Michael Abrashoft, USS *Benfold*

I know that in the real world there is proper protocol in nearly every place of work or service. A hierarchy, if you will. Of course we should respect position and office. And it is reasonable to expect those who report to you to acknowledge such. However, we have to remember that whatever we demonstrate to be more important is what they will focus on. So ask yourself, "Do I want people to care more about making me feel important, or are results what I really care about?"

If results are what you are looking for, pay more attention to the results. Make that the most important thing. It doesn't mean you have to give total disregard to office or position. In fact if you support and empower your people, you will find that they will have even more respect for you and your position.

Are You Showing the Way You Are Going?

"A leader is one who knows the way, goes the way, and shows the way."
—Maxwell

There are so many lessons in this one little quote by John Maxwell. The one I want to talk about today is showing the way.

Do you ever find yourself frustrated with your team? Is it as if they are all going in different directions and very few, if any, are going in the same general direction as you? As important as it is to know which way to go and actually go, the leader has to know how to show the way. Listen, if you don't learn how to effectively demonstrate AND communicate the direction you are going to your team, you will be frustrated to find them going in several directions. Most people want some level of structure and direction. And if they don't have some level of clarity, they will either pick a direction on their own or just muddle along until someone points in any direction.

Find a way to communicate not only the vision of where you are going but how you are going to get there. Take them on the journey with you by connecting with them and communicating with them. Develop a healthy relationship with them. Make it a priority that they understand how you intend to get where you are going. Let them be a part of the solution that gets you there. All they really want is to be a part, not apart.

Be blessed.

Who Gets Your Time?

"If they rarely ever 'need' your time, you probably need them.
If they seem to always 'need' your time, well…?"

—Frank Boudreau

The 80/20 Rule

The Pareto principle (also known as the 80/20 Rule) is the law of the vital few. Basically that means roughly 80 percent of the effects come from 20 percent of the causes. The principle originated from Italian economist Vilfredo Pareto in the late 1890s, when he said that 80 percent of the land was owned by 20 percent of the people and that 20 percent of his pea pods produced 80 percent of the peas. Since then many economists and management experts have observed the principle to hold true in many aspects, like:

- 80 percent of sales come from 20 percent of clients
- 80 percent of traffic jams happen on 20 percent of roads

- 20 percent of software code has 80 percent of the errors
- In sports 20 percent of the exercises and habits have 80 percent of the impact
- 20 percent of volunteers accomplish 80 percent of the work
- In factories 20 percent of the hazards account for 80 percent of the injuries
- 20 percent of the staff provide 80 percent of the impact

OK, so where am I going with this? Well, let's think about who and what is getting your time. You likely have been through some "time management" training of some kind. My favorite is Covey's "schedule the big rocks" principle. I love things that are easy to remember, like focusing on the big rocks or the 80/20 rule. In fact the two are connected, but Covey focuses on "what" gets your time. I want to focus on "WHO" gets your time.

Considering the 80/20 rule again, 80 percent of workplace drama comes from 20 percent of employees. On the other hand, 80 percent of workplace problems and challenges are solved by 20 percent of the employees. Now which 20 percent are you spending 80 percent of your time with? If your minutes and hours were cash, where would you want to invest it? Which 20 percent is going to bring you the greatest value and return?

Typically, your best and most productive employees "need" the least amount of your time. And your bottom performers "consume" the greatest amount. I'm not saying you should ignore the bottom performers or any others, for that matter. What I am saying is be smart with your time and invest it wisely. Invest in your top performers. Don't take them for granted. If you give them "real" time, intentional time, valuable time, you will benefit, they will benefit, and the whole team will benefit. Make it a priority to sacrifice a portion of your busy, crazy schedule for them. It will be your best investment. In fact you can't afford not to because if you neglect them they might feel that you really don't need them. And typically your top performers are less interested in "atta boys" and more interested in knowing that they are making a difference. And hey, if you need any help with how to start having those intentional conversations, let me know. I'd be glad to help get you started.

Are You Adding Value to Others?

Lately I have read a lot of passages in books and posts about adding value to people. I absolutely love this thought and strive to do so myself. But one day during my studies I had a challenging thought and question. How do I know if I am really adding value to someone?

You see, aside from being a student and teacher of leadership development, I am also a student and teacher of process improvement. Now in that arena we also talk about value. Value-added or non-value-added activity. In manufacturing value-added activity is described as any activity or process that "changes" the form, fit, or function of the product. It is also defined by the perspective of the customer. Would the customer be willing to pay for it? Everything else is non-value added.

That got me thinking about adding value to people. Is it really adding value to someone if it doesn't initiate or support positive changes in the person? And would that person consider it "value added"?

So are you truly adding value to the people you are trying to impact?

Why Would They Change?

Do you have an employee or a team member who leaves you frustrated at the lack of productivity?

Consider this hypothetical example. You have a couple of dozen employees. Yet you find yourself doing tasks they should be taking care of. In fact by the end of the typically long day you are exhausted from trying to get your stuff done as well as taking up the slack of your team. Sound familiar?

Perhaps it isn't that extreme for you. Or maybe you are just used to it. So at what point do you ask yourself why? Why do you find yourself doing tasks that members of your team should be doing? Well, to answer that question you'll probably need to ask a couple of more questions.

Is it the whole team that isn't productive, or just a couple?

When a team member doesn't perform, what are the consequences, if any?

To answer the original question—why would they change?—their reward is they get to relax while things get done for them. Now if in answering the latter two questions you determine that accountability is the key, chances are you are right. But let's not stop there. Let's keep asking. If this has been an ongoing problem, if you or other team members have been picking up the slack for quite a while, where does the change really need to happen? Well, it all starts with leadership so let's start with looking at ourselves. Back to more questions:

Am I being accountable for getting things done?

Am I showing up on time?

Do I follow up and follow through consistently?

Am I communicating my expectations clearly?

Am I consistent with my expectations?

We have to improve if we want our team to improve. So let's get to the root of the problem and work on us.

Let's go to work. Be blessed (Galatians 6:1–5).

Hard to Watch

"If you want to see them fly, don't rob them of their growth opportunity."

—Frank Boudreau

Chances are you have heard about how the struggles the baby bird goes through in the final minutes in the egg while trying to break through the shell are critical to its ability to fly and flourish. Experts say that without that struggle the muscles needed to one day fly won't develop properly and can leave the bird grounded.

Now honestly, watching one of those little guys struggle to break through the shell leaves me slightly torn. Part of me wants to help. Even if only a little bit to help it get started. I mean I know I shouldn't do all the work for him because of what we said earlier. But you know, just give it a little head start. That shouldn't hurt him at all, right? There's no telling how long it might take and I don't want to miss it. And if I give it just a little boost, I'll be able to watch the rest and I won't miss a thing.

Translate that to watching your child struggle to take their first steps. Of course there's no hard and fast absolute to when a child will take their first steps. And most pediatricians will encourage you to focus on the progress more than the timing of the child's early development. Because every strain to lift the head, every physical struggle to push themselves up to hands and knees, every attempt failed or successful to pull themselves up to their feet creates a demand on the muscles. This demand is processed by the body and generates a response to increase muscle strength and improve the motor skills. Without the struggles there are no demands. Without the demands there is no response to develop physically. Essentially if you hold your baby 24-7 and don't allow those struggles to occur, much like the baby bird, you are not helping the baby and are actually hurting them. I should add that, of course, you will "show" your child how to do things. But then you have to let them struggle while they try it themselves so that the necessary development occurs.

Let's move on to the preteen and teen years. When they reach those years there is a whole new dynamic to development. Social and relational challenges abound. And even though the details of these struggles are all over the map, everyone is met with challenges in these areas. Again as parents we have a desire to save our child from every struggle. It hurts to see them hurt and we want to protect them. We should protect them from unhealthy harm. But not the healthy struggle. The mother hawk will protect the egg from the predator, but will allow the struggle of breaking through the shell. Parenting youngsters is a delicate balance of protecting from the predators and allowing the struggles. Coaching them through relationship issues so they learn how to deal with them is essential. If you swoop in every time and "fix it," they won't learn. If they don't learn how to solve relationship issues in adolescence, they won't know how as adults in the working world.

So what about being a leader in the working or ministry world. The details of the challenges may change, but the principles stay the same. Are you protecting, or are you preventing? When do you step in and when do you step back? It's a balance. And you aren't going to get it right every time, but don't let that stop you from leading. Everyone fails. It's part of being a leader, just like it's part of being an athlete. Michael Jordan missed more than 9,000 shots in his career. He failed over 9,000 times yet he was arguably the best of all time. Edison found more than a thousand ways a light bulb wouldn't work, yet he was one of the greatest minds of modern history. Anyway back to the point. When you really care about the people you lead you don't want to see them struggle. You hurt when they hurt and you are tempted to go in and "fix it" for them all the time. But you have to stop and think first. Discernment is developed as we work out when to step in and when to step back. So let me share a key insight that has helped me develop in this area.

I ask myself:

Is there something they can learn from working through the problem themselves?
Do I have the understanding and experience to coach them through resolving it?
If not, do I know someone who does and can?

Be blessed.

Who Is Doing the Thinking?

Just how much do you want your team to depend on you? Of course everyone has an internal desire to be needed. We want to know that we are making a real contribution to those we lead. That's human nature. But have you considered making more than a contribution to your team? What if you could give them the priceless gift of not "needing" you? I know, that just sounds weird, right? Why would you want them to not need you? Isn't the whole point of leading is that the team needs you to "lead" them? Well, yes, the team does need you to lead. But in what way? Let me explain.

A big part of your responsibility as a leader is to solve problems. That doesn't really go away. And chances are that you have some ability to solve them and that might be part of the reason why you were selected to be the leader. But at what level should you be solving problems? Which problems should you be getting involved in? Oftentimes a leader finds themselves constantly solving problems. I know I've certainly been there. When we find ourselves there we need to stop for a moment and think about the problems we are solving and ask ourselves a question. Should I be solving this, or should they?

If you find yourself constantly solving problems, there could be several issues but I want to focus on one for the moment. That issue is that your team needs to learn "how" to solve problems. So the solution to that is to ask more questions and give fewer suggestions. Yes, suggest less, ask more. Consider some of these examples:

- What are your thoughts on this problem?
- What do you think contributed to the problem?
- How would you recommend approaching the situation?
- What would be the best way to approach this?
- What are some ideas on what we can do about this?

Ask questions that lead the person to think more. Ask questions that open up their thought process, not questions that "lead" their thoughts. If you are leading their thoughts to come up with a solution that you wanted, they aren't really thinking for themselves. And if you always do the thinking for them, you will always "have" to solve their problems for them. Don't put thoughts in their minds; help them with the thinking process. Encourage exploration for understanding. Help them learn how to gain understanding so they can explore possible solutions. Help them understand the actual boundaries of the situation so they consider all sides of the issue before making a decision.

Then comes the really hard part, letting them make the decision and letting them own the decision and the consequences. If you will coach them and teach them how to think through and solve problems, they won't need you to do it all the time. You will be amazed at how much energy and time it will free up for you so that you can focus on the bigger picture, which is what the team really needs from you as the leader.

Be blessed.

Developing Relationships

When the Real Leader Speaks

"The Law of E.F. Hutton, when the real leader speaks, people listen."

—John Maxwell

You may hold the "position" or title, but that doesn't necessarily mean that they will "listen" or truly hear everything you say.

The proof of real leadership is found in the followers. When you speak, do people really listen, or do they wait for someone else to speak before they engage?

The next time you are in a meeting and someone asks a question, observe the rest of the room to see who everyone looks to for an answer. In most cases that is the person they look to as the leader in that particular arena. Real leaders don't necessarily need to have a title to be heard.

"Leadership is influence, nothing more, nothing less."
"Positional leaders influence other positional leaders.
True leaders influence everyone in the room."

—John Maxwell

Nearly every time a person starts a new leadership role they aren't the real leader at first. There is usually another person already in the organization who is the real leader. If you find yourself in that new position, don't worry about it. Observe the folks around you and begin to develop relationships, especially with the ones to whom people are listening. Be consistent, straightforward, and patient. It takes time to develop the relationships and to show what you are made of. When you are getting started in a leadership position people are watching to see how you will hold up under pressure and to see the strength of your character. In time, if you are a leader, influence will come and people will listen. Until then you will need a little help from the other leaders to get things done.

If you've been in a leadership role for some time and you feel that you aren't being heard by those you lead, look inward first. Sit down with another leader you respect and trust, and seek advice on areas that need some work. Really try to figure out what it is that you are missing that is keeping you from being the "real" leader. Take the initiative to develop your leadership skills and learn from other leaders who have already developed in the areas that you need help in. Even the greatest leaders of our time and times past need counsel from time to time from other leaders regardless of the position held. In fact quite often some of the people these great leaders seek counsel from don't carry a "leadership title" at all.

So if leadership is influence, I would like to challenge us all to a level of influence that is generated from things like character, example, caring, trust, experience, and knowledge. Then eventually we will be able to say, "When we speak, people listen."

"Servant Leadership"…How Does that Work?

"From now on, any definition of a successful life must include serving others."

—President George Bush

"True leadership must be for the benefit of the followers, not the enrichment of the leaders."

—Robert Townsend

I truly admire the leader who has come up through the ranks to one day find themselves leading in the same arena they once followed. There are many challenges to overcome when you find yourself leading those who were once your peers. I also have much admiration for those who step into an organization as a leader because of previous experiences and education. A very different set of challenges are faced and will have to be overcome. It takes time to develop the relationships and trust level needed to lead. In either case there is much to learn, none of which can be learned in a day.

Today I want to talk about one of the most critical yet underestimated characteristics of a good leader, "servant attitude." Now an often-asked question is, "How can I have a servant's attitude and still be a leader?" Well, first we can't confuse a servant's attitude with being a doormat. In fact, it takes a lot of strength to be a good leader and have a servant's heart. Let me explain.

A servant's heart says:

"I will fulfill my duties as a leader because that's what is required of me."

"I will continue to learn and grow as a leader because those who follow me deserve a better leader."

"Those who follow me are far more important to me than I am and I will work hard to provide good direction."

"The recognition of my team is more important that my own recognition."

"I am here to provide support, direction, help, instruction, and wisdom for my team."

"I am here for them, not myself."

"I am willing to make the tough decisions and have the difficult conversations, so they don't have to."

Always remember, without a team to follow a leader is just a person standing alone. Without them you aren't a leader at all. To be a strong servant leader it comes down to the heart. You have to determine in your heart to put them first. The caring can be the driving force to put in the hard work. When you choose to make their growth, development, success, and productivity more important than your own, you find the motivation to push through the difficult, challenging, and sometimes awkward times. It becomes the energy to do more because you are working for something greater than yourself.

Challenge yourself; learn to serve your people by leading well.

Respect Given as a Gift

"Giving respect is an obligation, not a favor: it is an act of maturity, birthed in a profound understanding of Grace."

—Gary Thomas, author

Here are a couple of questions for you.

Why is it that we naturally respect a soldier in uniform? Why is it so easy to have so much respect for a firefighter?

I think we all have heard that if you want respect, you have to "earn it." I agree with that statement. However, is it possible that we have that statement so engrained in our thinking that we expect others to "earn" our respect? In fact it is likely that at times we actually demand that others "earn" our respect. We aren't going to just give our respect to anyone who comes along. I will talk about "earning" respect later, but for now I want to focus on **giving** respect.

Let's get back to the soldier and firefighter. It is so easy for us to respect them because of the sacrifice and bravery that their jobs demand from those who wear the uniform. They put themselves in harm's way to save and protect the innocent and hurting. I have the utmost respect for those who selflessly serve our country, here at home and abroad, civil service and military service. I believe these people "earn" our respect every day and I'm sure you would agree. We don't know much about them personally. We don't know what their personal hang-ups are. We don't know what their character flaws are when they are out of that uniform, but we still respect them. I'm not taking away from the honor and valor of what they do, but let's face it: it's pretty easy to respect them, isn't it? Whether we are five or 105 years old we respect them.

Now giving respect to those all around us every day can be a little more difficult. We know these people, some more than others. We know some of the hang-ups and character flaws. Well, guess what? We also have hang-ups and character flaws. Giving respect when we feel like others haven't earned it takes maturity. I'm not talking about condoning improper behavior; I'm talking about being respectful whether we think someone has "earned" it or not. That takes confidence and character, and as mature leaders leading by example we are obligated to do so.

I want to leave you with a couple of more questions.

What if we gave our respect to others as a gift and didn't expect anything in return? What if we gave others respect in spite of some hang-ups and character flaws?

My experience has been that the mass majority to whom I give respect return it in abundance. There will always be someone who doesn't respect others regardless of the circumstances. But let's not structure our behavior based on the very few. Honestly it takes guts to "give" respect with no expectation of returned respect. You have to be fearless. You have to be very confident in who you are and not be moved by unwarranted opinion.

So be brave, give the invaluable gift of respect. I believe you will find that the reward is much greater than the risk.

Who Do They Say You Are?

"The highest compliment leaders can receive is the one that is given by the people who work for them."
—*Leadership Inspirational Quotes & Insights for Leaders*, p. 109

All our lives we sought compliments and appreciation from our peers and our leaders. When we were kids we looked for it from our parents and teachers. When we were teenagers it was our friends and our parents (probably mostly our friends). When we entered the working world it was our coworkers and our bosses. When we became parents we looked for compliments from our parents and other parents. Hmmm… Have you taken a chance and asked your kids how well they think you are doing as a parent? Chances are they are going to tell you that you are a good parent and you are doing a good job. The real question is, what do your kids say to their friends about you when you aren't around? Oh boy, that's a tough one. Well, the same can apply to us as leaders but it is sometimes difficult for us to shift gears that way.

So what do your employees say about you? Better yet, what do they say to others about you when you aren't around? Would they describe you using the words that you listed as the top ten qualities of a leader?

It might be difficult to get to the bottom of that truth, but if you will hear their hearts you just might find some lifesaving nuggets that will help you grow. You can't take offense and you have to consider the context from which the info came to you. As I said in regard to giving respect it takes guts to go this route. You have to provide a safe environment for them to give you that kind of feedback. And you have to be ready for some really tough truths sometimes. But consider this: their perception of you is their reality of you. And even if their perception is based on part and not the whole picture, their perception is at least partially your reality whether you know it or not. And if you don't know it, you can't fix it. So again be brave and be humble and see if you can get some of that real feedback of how you are truly doing as a leader in their eyes. If you are genuine, and they are honest, and you take it seriously, it can dramatically improve your ability to lead.

The risk is great but the reward is even greater.

What Can We Learn from a Flock of Geese?

I'm discovering new things about leadership in the strangest of ways and rediscovering old things about leadership in odd ways as well.

One afternoon my wife and I were on the motorcycle on our way to a dinner ride and I saw several flocks of geese. It's a fairly common site this time of year, as they are coming back up from the south as the warm, moist air returns.

As I was watching they were flying in their typical V shape in their usual orderly fashion. However, one of the flocks seemed to have just taken off from a pit stop at a local pond so they weren't quite in their formation yet when I first spotted them. I was simply astounded as I watched them get into formation. What surprised me was how each one moved into position. It wasn't at all like I expected it to happen. I expected them to start out in a big blob in the sky and simply stack up in the closest available slot, or slide into place one behind the other until they were all in line. But that wasn't what happened at all. In fact they would come from one side of the group to the other to get into their spot. It was almost as if they each knew exactly which spot they were supposed to be in, and that was exactly where they each flew to. The kicker was watching the last one get into place. It wasn't that he was late getting off the ground and just slipped into the last spot in line. As a matter of fact his spot was so clearly open it was amazing. The V shape formed fairly quickly but there was a vacant spot about four geese up from the tail end of the left side of the V. It was the exact amount of even spacing left open for that goose. The ones behind the vacant spot didn't move up and make him get in the back. They didn't even shift over until he got there. They were in their specific spots in perfect formation and simply held his spot open for him until he arrived. And as surely as that spot was left open and ready for him, he quickly caught up to the group and slipped into his spot as they flew overhead.

That brief little wildlife observation left me momentarily speechless. Yeah, I know, I'm a little weird. But it was just really cool to watch. Anyway there are so many things we can learn from that illustration.

1. Sometimes we are leaders simply because we know and understand our position at the moment and don't jump into someone else's slot just because they are a little late getting there.

2. If we do jump into that slot we are still in a long line if we are trying to get to the very front. Know this, that guy in the very front gets 100 percent of the headwind, rain, and dust and is sometimes flying blind in the clouds, navigating by instinct. So if you are going to take that position you need to be strong, tough, be able to let the water roll of your back, and you better have a lot of wisdom and experience because there will be a lot of leaders following you if you are the head goose and they will be counting on you to provide direction, wisdom, and a wind draft they can get into.

3. If we jump into that slot just because the other guy had a slow day or was a little slow out of the gate, that same guy just might step right over you when he gets his momentum back. However, if you hold his spot open for him and even help him get back in line, when your time does truly come that same guy will likely slide over and make room for you and maybe even cheer you on as you do.

4. Each step forward you take in line should stretch you and challenge you and make you a little stronger, a little wiser, a little more patient. All of which will help prepare you for the next step, and each step will ultimately prepare you for that front spot in time.

Remember if you think you are leading but nobody is behind you, you are just a lonely goose flying around all by yourself.

Measure Twice, Cut Once

"Measure twice cut once."

—English proverb

Most of us have heard this saying many times, but if not it simply refers to double-checking our measurements before we cut something to prevent wasting material. That makes sense, doesn't it? Especially if we cut something too short. Once we cut something we really can't uncut it. This is one of the most basic principles in manufacturing. If you do make a mistake, you might be able to weld or epoxy or glue it back together but it will not be quite the same. If you work in the glass business, you know that there is nothing you can do to glue it back together. Once it is cut, that's it. No going back.

OK, OK, I'll get to the point. Once we say something we can't unsay it, right? Sometimes we wish we could take it back, but we can't. Sure we can apologize and we might be forgiven. We all need grace, but it has been said. And if the damage is severe, the relationship might never be the same. So let's employ that same principle to our speech. The tongue is often referred to as a sword. And it has the ability to destroy if not kept in check. It can also be referred to as a scalpel and be used as an instrument to bring healing. So let's measure twice and cut once. Let's double check our intents before speaking. Let's use our speech to bring healing instead of pain. The only time to use the sword should be to defend the weak against the enemy.

Do You Really Believe in What You Are Putting Out There?

"What convinces is conviction. You must believe in the argument you are advancing."

—Lyndon Johnson, former US president

If you are speaking a message, teaching a lesson, preaching a sermon, or leading a charge, and nobody seems to believe or follow you, you might need to ask yourself this question: Do I really believe what I am putting out there?

If the answer is no or even not sure, you then need to ask why. The truth is that if you don't believe the message you are putting out there, people just won't follow you in that direction. But if you do believe in what you are putting out there and do with conviction, people will likely follow. And when they do, remember that you have a great responsibility for your message or charge. So make sure you check the moral compass before you blaze that trail.

If you do believe your message and feel good about your moral compass and still have difficulty getting people to listen, check your level of conviction in what your message is. It is possible to believe what you're saying without having real conviction in it. Dig deep and try to remember why you began your journey to begin with. Find your passion and allow that to come through the message. Conviction becomes contagious. If you really believe it, there is a pretty good chance they will as well.

Be blessed and lead well.

Are You a Learner?

"Leadership and learning are indispensable to each other."

—John F. Kennedy

Traditionally when we reach a point of leadership we feel that we should have the answers. And it's easy to reach that conclusion because we find that people are coming to us for help, advice, direction, and the like. Chances are we are trying to live up to the example of someone we looked up to who seemed to have all the answers and assume that means we should, too.

The truth is, the leaders who have the most real answers are the ones who have the best learning habits. The essence of leading is forging ahead. Leading people to a place they haven't yet been. To continue to lead you must continue to learn. And a good learner can learn something from anyone or any circumstance.

Can I Have Your Attention Please?

"Give whatever you are doing and whoever you are with the gift of your attention."

—Jim Rohn

As leaders we are involved in many things. And we are involved in many conversations. We are also responsible for staying in contact with those we lead and those who lead us. And we communicate in many ways, most of which are tied to the electronics we carry around. How many times have we tried to have a serious conversation with someone only to be interrupted by a call or text or email? By our phone or theirs?

The truth is, there are all kinds of books or classes on communication and ways to phrase things or package a message for your audience. But the most valuable form of communication for a leader is the skill of listening. As leaders we are pretty good at telling or explaining or maybe even teaching. But we HAVE to be good at listening. If we don't learn how to effectively listen to our team we are essentially going it alone.

So the next time you are having a conversation with a member of your team put your phone on silent. Ignore it for the conversation. Trust me, you can't afford not to. Also learn good listening habits like eye contact and nonverbal responses like a nod. Give feedback to let the person know you hear them and understand.

Do We Condemn or Forgive?

"Any fool can criticize, condemn, and complain but it takes character and self-control to be understanding and forgiving."
—Dale Carnegie

The other day my son said, "Dad, as long as I can remember these people have criticized you and accused you of having hidden motives. How can you not be mad at them for how they've treated you?" I replied, "Son, they criticize what they don't understand. They don't understand true genuine caring and concern while taking a stand for what is right."

It's easy to get defensive when someone wrongs you. It's easy to react and justify the need to "get them back." Anyone can do that because it's a natural reaction.

But how about we take a different road? Let's go against our nature and see beyond the offense. Let's gain an understanding of what causes people to do things that might hurt. Let's look at their hearts instead of their actions. Let's remember that we, too, have done wrong and said wrong things and needed forgiveness and understanding. And let's remember that we will likely need it again.

Be blessed.

Do You Really Care? 'Cause They Might Not

"No one cares how much you know, until they know how much you care."
—Theodore Roosevelt

As leaders we assume that the whole reason we are in the position we are in is because of what we know. Therefore it must be that we should tell people what we know. In fact we tend to jump out there and tell people right away.

Look, there are lots of reasons why we end up in leadership positions. For example, elected, appointed, to fill a vacancy, effort and reward. Regardless of how we found ourselves in the leadership position we are in, what counts is what we do once we get there. Now that we have clarified that let's talk about the "now what?"

Our people are generally ready to hear good instruction and direction. But first they have to trust you. It's the same for you, right? You aren't going to follow someone without first knowing you can trust them, right? Well, it's the same for the folks who follow you. It's your job to develop the relationships with the people you lead. Leading by "position" will only get you so far. Leading by "permission" is what takes you the distance. Let your people know you care about them. Work for them, know them, earn their trust. Then they will be ready to hear what you have to say. And far more likely to act on your instructions.

Leave It Better Than You Found It

"I never pick up an item without thinking of how I might improve it."

—Thomas A. Edison

I remember a time many years ago when our kids were little, I had borrowed a pickup truck from a friend so that I could move some furniture. After we finished up one of my boys came along with me to return the truck. Along the way I stopped at the car wash. My son looked at me and asked, "What are we doing, Dad?" I answered, "Son, anytime I borrow something, I always try to return it in better shape than when I borrowed it." As any young boy would, he asked why. So I told him that it's simply the right thing to do. I told him how my friend worked really hard to earn the money to buy that truck and we were blessed with being able to use it. So in return for being able to use it, we were going to wash it and vacuum it and fill it up with gas so it would be nice and clean and ready for him to go anywhere. I remember borrowing a lawn mower once, and while I had it I did some work on it so that it would work better for the owner the next time he used it.

In today's society we are continually looking for what we will get out of things. We buy, borrow, or trade for something and use it up then discard it. Unfortunately, and usually unwittingly, we sometimes do that in relationships.

So to Edison's point, let's purpose in our hearts and minds to leave things better than we found them. Let's leave folks better than we found them. Let's add value to everything we touch and everyone we meet rather than taking away. Let's ask ourselves what we are bringing to our relationships. Are we adding more joy, or bringing sadness? Are we sharing wisdom to build things up, or simply opinions that tear things down? Are we adding, or subtracting? Think about your relationships right now. Think about three friends or coworkers you spend the most time with and ask yourself if you are adding or subtracting. Are you giving or taking? Are you encouraging or discouraging? Think about the last few conversations you had with someone in your household. Did you build up or tear down? Did you give or receive? Did you think about what they wanted, or what you wanted?

Here's the cool thing. No matter where you might be on the give-and-take scale you can always start today to improve it. But I'm not going to give you a five-step plan to making it better. I'm not going to give you a road map to better relationships. I'm simply going to talk about one thing, the heart. It's simply a heart thing. If you want to improve your level of positive impact on your relationships, it all boils down to matters of the heart. So do this. Check your heart motivation. Challenge yourself to examine yourself. And be gut-level honest with yourself. When something negative happens to you and your family, what is your first thought?

Is it how it's going to affect you? Or is it how it's going to affect them? When you have a misunderstanding with a friend, do you feel anger? Or do you feel regret? Are you thinking, "I can't believe they said that"? Or are you thinking, "I wonder what made them feel so bad that they said something like that"? I know this is a lot of feely-feely stuff, but do it anyway. Really dig deep to see where your heart is. Then challenge yourself to always bring more to a relationship than you take away. Try to walk away from every encounter leaving the room with more of something positive than when you entered.

Try to leave it better than you found it.

Be blessed.

Where Does Communication Rank in Your Top Ten List?

"If I went back to college again, I'd concentrate on two areas: learning to write and to speak before an audience.

Nothing in life is more important than the ability to communicate effectively."

—President Gerald Ford

Today more than ever, effective communication is critical to success in any arena. Whether it be parenting, management, ministry, team activities, or any job that requires interaction with others. Notice that I said "effective" communication. And that requires more than just talking.

Effective communication requires connecting to people. It means you have to understand them at some level and be able to relate to them. The ability to listen to people is a key factor to connecting as well as valuing them.

Look, at the end of the day, if you want to effectively communicate, you are going to have to get outside yourself. You are going to have to focus on the needs of others. Basically people don't care how much you know, until they know how much you care.

To effectively communicate, start listening and caring.

Be blessed.

Who Is This Really About?

"When you are trying to connect with people, it's not about you, it's about them."

—John C. Maxwell

Human nature lends itself to, well, self. We are basically born selfish. Let's face it. From the very moment we take our first breath we come into this world screaming me, me, me. And as a toddler we don't have to be taught how to say, "Mine."

Interestingly, though, if we truly want to connect with people, we need to make it about them. If you really want to connect with someone, you have to listen more and talk less. And when you do talk your statements and questions need to be more about them than yourself. If you want someone to be interested in you, you will need to show interest in them. So basically we have to fight our general nature and focus on the desires and needs of others.

Easier said than done, right? Be encouraged, and no matter how many times you blow it keep trying. It is very well worth it. The more you value them by putting them first, the more they will be willing to help you. And we all need help in order to be successful in any way.

Be blessed.

Are You Sure You Heard Right?

"Don't assume that people HEAR what you are THINKING."

—Frank Boudreau

Let's face it. We are super busy these days. Not just at work but in virtually every part of our lives. We have more conversations in a single day than we could possibly count. Face-to-face, one on one, meetings, phone calls, text messages, emails, Facebook, and I'm sure many other ways that I don't even know about. With all those conversations going on in a single day, and sometimes more than one at a time, exactly how clearly do we believe we are communicating when it really counts?

I'm sure you've heard the saying, "I'd rather do one or two things right than ten things wrong," or "I'd rather do one or two things 100 percent than ten things half complete." Let's consider doing the same thing with our conversations. Yes, some conversations are quick and passing and don't really require a lot of focus. But I bet far too often we let an important conversation turn into a quick-passing one because we "don't have time." Unfortunately when we let that happen the other person feels devalued. And often it drives the need for multiple conversations later just so that we can clear up the miscommunication left in the wake, which takes up much more time.

Learn to recognize an "important" conversation. Especially when it's important to the other person. Nothing shows respect as much as giving someone your "undivided" attention. It will also gain you respect in return.

Consider this:

- STOP – focus on them. Press the pause button on EVERYthing else going on for just a moment.
- TURN – to them, and let your body language say, "I'm listening to you right now."

○ LISTEN – to what they are saying. Repeat it back to them if necessary, saying, "What I heard you say was…"

○ SEEK – to understand. Make sure you clearly understand their questions or issues.

○ RESPOND – with clarity and make sure they actually understand, not just what you said but what you "meant."

Be clear and be blessed.

Change, Not Only What But Who

Its' been said, "Nothing is great, until a life is changed."

There are a lot of things that are "good." There is good food, good music, and good movie. We have good friends and we know good people and we hopefully had some good teachers growing up. We probably even know a lot of good leaders. But how many of any of these would you say are "great"?

Much like the weather here in Oklahoma, change is inevitable. In the continuous improvement world change is the business. And unfortunately sometimes change becomes the goal. Basically, change for the sake of change. So when I talk about change in this context please understand that I mean real change for the good. Positive change that brings value to those impacted by it.

So back to my question, how many of the things mentioned are truly "great"? Perhaps you have a favorite song that does so much more than make you tap your foot. It truly impacts you every time you hear it. Most likely you heard it at just the right time in your life, when it truly moved you and made you think about things differently. Much like a "great" movie that has a message that made you begin looking at something totally differently, in a good way.

What about being a "great" leader? Many leaders are "good" leaders who impact positive change in process and product, but what does it take to be a great leader? Well, if we put it into the context of the first statement, when you truly impact positive change in the people you lead you are on the doorstep of being a "great" leader.

Many Look, Few See

Have you ever gone to a popular vacation place, a place where everything around you is there for the tourism? Lights, colors, fancy clothes, signs, sounds, and smiling faces. So many things to look at, visual distractions everywhere to take your mind off the reality you left at home. You and every other tourist is looking all around trying to take in as much as possible.

But have you ever stopped in the middle of all that and looked to see what was in plain sight but hardly noticeable? I have done this a lot lately and realized that up to that point I was only looking and not seeing. There was another world right in front of me that I couldn't see because I was just looking. I wasn't trying to see. The tour guide trying to keep the bills paid while raising five kids. The homeless woman in the alley thirty feet from the lights and sounds. The stress in the eyes and behind the smile of the waiter because his wife is sick and they don't know if she's going to be okay.

The harsh reality was that I couldn't see that world because it wasn't my world, and the only world I was interested in. It wasn't until I was willing to SEE beyond myself that I was able to SEE what was right in front of me.

So here is my challenge. When you go to work or church or other usual spot, stop and look past yourself and try to see. See past the smile mustered up to shield the pain. See beyond the "Fine, how are you?" to see the frustration or disappointment. See beyond your world and into theirs. You just might make a breakthrough, or simply make a difference.

MANAGING YOUR TIME

Twenty-Four Hours in a Day Is All We Get, Spend It Wisely

Tom Landry once said that he had three priorities in life: God, family, and football—in that order. "Until you get your priorities straight you will never be truly successful at anything."

We each have twenty-four hours in a day and seven days in a week. No more, no less. Also we each have many things pulling on that time and being able to juggle them is a necessity. Often we find ourselves losing focus because we are trying to juggle too many things at once. When you find yourself scattered because of this it's always a good idea to stop for a little bit and let your mind settle. Then go back to the basics of your priorities, whatever they are, and make sure you have them identified clearly in your mind. Then take all these things that you are trying to juggle and filter them though your priorities. Take some time in doing this and be realistic with what you are making note of.

We each only have 100 percent of our time. When you break things down you might find that you have too many things that require, say, 20 percent of your time to be effective, and you are only able to give 10 percent of your time to each of those things. That basically means that the important things in your life might be getting a watered-down version of your best, which really isn't your best; it's just what you have left.

So what or who really isn't getting enough of you?

Loyalty Given Is Loyalty Earned

"You've got to give loyalty down, if you want loyalty up."

—Donald T. Regan

We all want to know that those we lead are loyal to us. We want to know that if the chips are down they have our backs, right?

The fact is that we need them to be loyal to us. We need to know that they won't turn their backs on us just because they don't quite understand a decision we made. We need to know that they will support us especially when times are tough.

I'm here to tell you that you can have that kind of loyalty, but it comes at a price. You have to GIVE that kind of loyalty. Your people have to know that you have THEIR backs when things get tough or you don't fully understand a decision they've made. I'm not talking about blind loyalty. I'm talking about a loyalty that comes with understanding. That kind of loyalty doesn't just happen. You have to develop RELATIONSHIPS with your people to get that kind of loyalty. They have to see you sacrifice a little. They have to see that you put others first, including but not exclusively them. They have to know that you are genuine and real. They have to know that your heart is in the right place. In short you have to earn it. You can't buy it from them. You can't order them to do it. They don't owe it to you just because you're their boss.

I can assure you that when loyalty is honestly earned it will be richly rewarded.

And I must add one of the best ways to model this is to show that kind of loyalty to your boss. Don't expect them to do something that you're not willing to do yourself. Trust me, they'll know if you are loyal to your boss.

What Is Stopping You from Completing Your Task?

"Neither snow, nor rain, nor gloom of night stays these couriers from the swift completion of their appointed rounds."

—The postman's creed

OK, I have come across this many times in books, in speeches, or even in movies. Each time I have heard it the point of valiant effort was being made, and rightfully so. But usually it was to point out a very public or heroic effort, until I read Cal Ripken Jr.'s book. Yes, Cal, the Iron Man of baseball, who holds the longest consecutive game streak in baseball. Not to mention his many, many other accomplishments in baseball. This guy could write a book on staying at it—oh wait, he did. Anyway he did talk about another great ballplayer, Lou Gehrig, who had an incredible streak of his own, but what caught my attention was the others he mentioned in his book.

He talked about "Herbert Christiansen, who had not missed a day of work since he'd begun the job back on April 1, 1936." And Ernie Tyler, who on Cal's two thousandth and one hundred thirty-first game was "working on his 2,180th straight game seated behind the backstop doing his job as the team's umpire attendant." Cal's comment about Ernie: "Talk about a quiet, dedicated guy; Ernie was the best."

How did they do it? Good question. I'm sure there were plenty of things in their lives that could have gotten in the way. But somehow they didn't let it. Cal, in a time when the average baseball career was less than six years, had a twenty-one-year career with the same team and almost never missed a game. And how about Ernie? That was a guy who didn't let things get in his way of commitment. And that really is the point I want to make about all this. I gotta tell you, things try to get in the way, stuff happens, life happens, and all too often we let those things stop us from completing our tasks. I'm certainly guilty from time to time.

So whether it be showing up for work every day or getting the report done, meeting the production goals, making it to the little league game, whatever commitments we make, we must fulfill them. Even the most repetitive or general tasks. Demonstrate to the people you lead at work and at home that no matter how far up the ladder you go the daily things still have to be done. If you want to do great things you must start, and continue, the small things. Michael Jordan didn't stop shooting free throws after he won his first championship. Tiger still hits the driving range every day.

Besides, what a powerful message to send to your kids. Dependability, reliability, consistency, steadfast. Let's tell our families, "You can count on me." In a world where the popular thing is to do what you feel like when you feel like, our families need to know the truth. So let's show them how to "get it done." Even when we don't "feel" like it.

Wait on the Lord

Psalm 27:14: "Wait for the LORD; be strong and take heart and wait for the LORD."

Learning how to wait on God's timing is a difficult thing to do.

As leaders we are conditioned to "lead," go first, take the first step, get out there in front, and so on. If you have been receiving these posts for very long, you have read some of the things I have written on the subject, such as the quote about pushing or pulling the string. We need to be willing to take that first step. After all how can we expect them to follow something we don't do?

As a believer I have tried for years to understand this psalm. What does it really mean to wait on the Lord? David gave us a very simple but very powerful truth.

Here is where I'm going with this.

Have you ever found yourself trying and trying to get through something and getting nowhere?

Have you ever been stumped on what the next move should be so you just tried one thing after the other and got little or no results?

Have you ever found yourself thinking, "I can usually solve this stuff. I usually know what to do here. Why not now?"

Often when these things happen we go to a mentor or colleague or close friend who's been there and done that to get advice on what to do. I certainly encourage you to do that. And sometimes that unlocks something and gets us unstuck, but not always.

Shifting gears for a moment, I believe that the Lord's timing is perfect. I also believe that in whatever He is doing He is doing several things at the same time. Have you ever noticed when something just strangely works out, how it did by several things happening at the same time in unbelievable timing? Pretty cool, huh? Well, I don't think that was just luck. God invented multitasking. Sorry Bill Gates, you weren't the first to think of it. The Lord is always doing many things all at the same time. That being said, He is perfect but we are not, and He usually does things in our lives through the people and situations around us.

OK, back to point. During the times we have talked about I believe that we are to patiently wait on the Lord and his timing. It could be that He is working on getting other things lined up in order to move on our behalf as well. So if we aren't getting anywhere, it could be that He is still getting things in order. That is when we wait, pay close attention, keep your eyes peeled, and watch for when the time is right. Then we move forward again. The difficult thing there is not stressing about it while we are waiting. That is where faith and trust in the Lord come into play. I'd be glad to talk on that some time.

Be blessed.

Put the Compass before the Clock

In today's hustle and bustle life we always seem to be struggling with time. In a nutshell we never have enough. Stephen Covey has some great teaching on time management that helps you categorize the things that you do into four basic quadrants. I won't take the time to cover all the material but I encourage you to search for this concept. It basically teaches that rather than always focusing on what's urgent, learn to focus a specific amount of time on what's important. And one of the most important things to focus on is your direction or your plan to get where you are going. Spend intentional time deciding what direction you are going in and how you want to get there.

I said all that to say that it is vitally important to know where you are going before you hit the gas. Otherwise you might end up going the wrong way really fast.

Are You Getting Sidetracked?

"Every moment you spend addressing a critic is a valuable moment that you take away from your dream."

—Steve Harvey

No matter what your dreams or goals are there will always be a critic or two giving their two cents about you, or your dreams, or how you are pursuing your dreams. The criticism comes from many sources. Perhaps they have their own fears of failure and are afraid that you are going to fail, too. Perhaps they feel stuck and can't bear the thought of you leaving them behind. It could also just be good ole-fashioned jealousy. Whatever the case you can't judge your progress based on the opinions of others. It's your dream, not theirs. So don't let their fears become yours.

Will you fail? Absolutely! Will you have setbacks and disappointment? You can count on it! Look, if you aren't making mistakes it's only because you're not doing anything different. And the only way you get a different result than what you've already been getting is by doing something different than what you've been doing. If you are doing something new, you are going to make mistakes. OK, so make them, learn from them, then move on. It's the only way you grow. And by growing you are doing what you need to do to reach your dreams.

So don't waste your time on someone else's thoughts about YOUR dreams. Spend your valuable time working toward the dream.

Be blessed.

Finishing the Year Well

I have a couple of mentors who still speak into my life. Through these mentors, Dave and John, I learned to develop a habit of setting aside at least a day. That's a whole day, morning to night. Not just a couple of hours. To turn off everything, and I mean everything, and just think. Think about the year and how things went. Kind of like finishing up a project and saying what went well and what didn't. What did I learn new and what did I wish I had learned? Since I began doing this about ten years ago it has changed my life. I have become far more productive. My focus and purpose is so much more clear. And as I am a forever work in progress I will continue to do this for the rest of my life.

If you don't already do this, I want to encourage you to give it a try this year. I promise you if you commit the time it will be one of the best decisions you make.

Below are some of the questions my mentors have shared with me:

How can I serve my team better in the coming year?

What do I want my team to know and act upon?

What wears you out and what energizes you?

How can I model the behaviors that I want to see in them?

What can I do this year to grow as a leader?

Be blessed.

OTHERS DEVELOPING YOU

Seek Good Counsel—You Won't Regret It

My brother in the Lord posted this scripture on Facebook and it hit me square in the eyes:

Proverbs 11:14: "Where no counsel is, the people fall: but in the multitude of counsellors there is safety."

First of all, let me preface this by saying the counsel you seek should be GOOD counsel. What is good counsel? I'm glad you asked. The best way to determine if someone can give good counsel is by their fruit. What I mean by that is, if you are seeking counsel about, say, a marriage issue, look for someone you trust and has solid evidence of a good marriage. I wouldn't seek counsel on marriage issues from someone who doesn't have a healthy respect for their spouse and talks negatively about marriage all the time. That person will likely lead you down the wrong path. If it is a business issue, look for someone who has a solid approach to business and has evidence of success in that area. It doesn't mean they've never had problems. It just means they seem to know how to deal with the problems they have faced and might be able to help you face them as well.

Simply put, they can't lead you where they've never been.

Another key aspect of good counsel is someone who will tell you what you NEED to hear, not just what you WANT to hear. A real friend will be willing to tell you the tough stuff. They will be willing to step out of the comfort zone and give it to you straight. Let's face it. There is enough watered-down, misty-eyed hot air floating around. You don't need that from a true friend and counsel.

Back to the original point. Being without any counsel is a dangerous place to be. Everyone, regardless of position, needs good counsel. Nobody knows everything. If you never seek good counsel you are a sitting duck. Attacks and failures can be lurking around any corner.

I've heard some say, "I seek counsel in the Lord and that's all the counsel I need." Well, I completely agree with that statement. But I think it is important to know that the Lord often provides that counsel through people He places in our lives. Remember in the beginning He said that it is not good for man to be alone. Walking through this life alone with no counsel is a dangerous and lonely thing. And if you're going to find someone to talk to about stuff, you might as well look for someone who can truly direct you in a positive way. And if you are a believer in the Lord, ask Him to help you recognize the ones He has placed in your life for directing you where you need to go.

Let's be real. Anybody can give bad advice. There is more than enough of that going around. Don't waste your time on it. Take the time to seek out GOOD counsel.

Be blessed.

Constructive Feedback Is Critical to Leading

"It takes humility to seek feedback, but it takes wisdom to understand it, analyze it, and take appropriate action."

—Stephen R. Covey

You have most likely heard me talk about how important it is to have someone in your inner circle who will tell you what you NEED to hear instead of what you **want** to hear. Someone who will give you the real truth and will let you know when you are blowing it. Of course it should be someone committed to your success, someone you can trust.

Well, hearing it is only half of it. Hearing the truth doesn't do you any good if you don't do anything about it. Once you hear the tough stuff it's time to do something with it. Try this:

1. Give it some real thought. Be gut-level honest with yourself. Be realistic and see if there is anything there that you can at least identify with. One check is if it hurts your feelings or ego a bit, there is probably something to work on.
2. Seek good counsel on how you can make adjustments or changes to improve or correct it. Sometimes the person who pointed out the issue doesn't know how to correct it, and that's OK. It doesn't mean the problem doesn't exist. If there are any doubts, get another point of view.
3. Do something about it. Take action and make the correction. At the end of the day, if you don't take any action, things won't change and you will only get frustrated at best and you might lose a friend or worse.

Look, nobody is perfect. We all need to make adjustments along the way. It is called growing and we all need to do it regardless how far along we are. Take action and be blessed.

What Are We Thinking?

"Of course we become what we think about.
The question is, Do we know what we are thinking about?"
—Steve Siebold

My pastor once asked, "Do you have to work at getting bad thoughts to come to your mind?" Of course the answer is no. The truth is we have to work at making sure we focus on good thoughts. Negative thinking kind of creeps up on us sometimes, and if we don't recognize them and push them out of our minds we can certainly find ourselves in a bit of a cloud. Left unattended that can actually lead to depression.

You might say that negative things are just part of leading and that's the way it is. Well, that is true, but how we think about and respond to those negative things are our choice. You might also ask, what's the big deal? I'll get through it somehow. You probably will. The question I ask is, how many casualties will there be in the end? If we approach everything with negative thought and speech, we will have a terribly negative impact on our team and we might even lose them altogether.

So it is imperative that we approach every situation with positive thinking and speech, so that our team can have some confidence and hope in what is to come and will want to get behind us and help with the solutions.

And if you do find yourself in a struggle with negative thinking that you can't seem to shake, talk to a trusted peer. Someone who can handle the fact that you are struggling and give you POSITIVE feedback and encouragement. Even if it means a swift kick in the pants, with love and respect of course.

Be blessed.

Are You Being Coached?

"Great coaching is helping people discover what they already know."

—Bill Gove, 1912–2001

The greatest athletes in the world have coaches. One of my favorites, Jerry Rice, had a coach. Michael Jordan had a coach. Michael Phelps had a coach. Lance Armstrong had a coach. The list goes on.

Back to my favorite Jerry Rice. His former coaches and teammates are often asked what they thought of Jerry's dedication to practice. All would talk about how dedicated he was and how hard he worked even during the off-season. Even with his high skill level and natural talent he worked hard. What I thought was very interesting, though, was the fact that his former coaches talk about how coachable he was. Jerry was a student first and athlete second. Typically the great ones are all very coachable, which basically means that they seek out people who can teach them something about the game that they don't know and they will listen and put into practice what they learn. They never reach a point where they say, "That's it, I know all I can know about what I do." The great ones know that they can never know it all. There is always more to learn.

John Maxwell says that teachability is one of *The 21 Indispensable Qualities of a Leader.*

It's true that a self-motivated person can continue to grow. But at what pace? Is it taking much longer than expected? The fact is that we all need a little coaching from time to time, some help from someone who has been there and done that. We should be looking for people we can learn from. Please remember, though, it's better to give than to receive. Be ready to give of yourself. Be ready to serve in some capacity the person you seek to learn from. Chances are that person will learn something from you as well.

So get out there and get connected to people. Spend some time with someone who has been there and done that. Who knows? We just might learn something that will save us some serious headaches down the road.

Be blessed.

Motivation or Inspiration?

Hmmm, do we need motivation or do we need inspiration? Wow, what a question. I suppose you might say that it depends on the individual. Are you typically inspired to do something, or are you motivated to do something?

Well, let's think about this for a minute. Motivation can come in many forms, but basically it is something that urges movement in some way. A ball is motivated by a foot. A predator is motivated by hunger pains to seek out its prey. A sharp object in your chair can motivate you to stand up rather quickly. Now inspiration is something different. The literal meaning of inspiration is "to be breathed in…" The Word, or the Bible, is God-inspired or God-breathed.

Motivation is the energy that moves something; inspiration is the dream that gives direction to the motivation.

Motivation is the push and the urgency. Inspiration is the desire and the duration.

In simple truth we need both. We need the motivation, which can take many forms like need, pain, fear, hunger, and the like. So that is what gets us moving. The inspiration is the direction like desire, a dream, a hope. It is what guides us and gives us the ability to go the distance when the initial energy is gone. It is what keeps us moving forward in the right direction toward the dream.

Inspiration is about possibilities. So consider the possibilities of achieving your dream. Allow yourself to be motivated and inspired. Look for things that will motivate, but also listen for things that inspire you to move toward your dream.

Be blessed.